HEREFORDSHIRE

J. W. Tonkin

HEREFORDSHIRE

B. T. Batsford Ltd

London

First published 1977
Copyright J. W. Tonkin 1977

Photoset by Weatherby Woolnough,
Wellingborough, Northants
Printed by The Pitman Press, Bath
for the publishers B. T. Batsford Ltd
4 Fitzhardinge Street, London W1H 0AH
ISBN 0 7134 0576 7

Contents

Illustrations

Acknowledgements

The Author and Publishers would like to thank the following for their permission to reproduce the illustrations in this book: Peter Baker Photography, nos 2, 5, 10, 13; Barnaby's Picture Library, nos 19, 20; A. F. Kersting, F.R.P.S., nos 1, 6, 7, 9, 15, 16, 17, 21, 22, 23, 24; Kenneth Scowen, F.R.P.S. F.I.I.P., nos 3, 4, 8, 11, 14, 18; Spectrum Colour Library, no. 12.

To Muriel

Introduction

The writer and his wife first saw Herefordshire on a bitter January afternoon during the snow and frost of the winter of 1963. They drove into the county from the east across the river Teme and up the hill over Bringsty Common, past the woods of Brockhampton to Bromyard. In those days, before the by-pass was built, the road ran through the main street where the lights were going up and the black-and-white of the timber-framed houses seemed to belong to the snow-covered landscape. It was warm and welcoming.

So was Leominster, when half an hour later they slid down the last hill and over the Lugg into the town. Next day it was on to Wigmore, Weobley, then back to Canon Pyon and so to Hereford through banks of snow on either side of the road. There lay the city down in the Wye valley ringed by hills, with away to the west the Black Mountains, white in their winter covering, a long line guarding the county.

Later that day, more lights and more timber-framing at dusk at Ledbury and then over the Malverns, the eastern guardians of Herefordshire and out to the vale of Severn and lowland England.

In that 24 hours much of what makes the county had been seen, perhaps more important, felt. The fertile river valleys, the ring of hills surrounding the county, the ups and downs and twists and turns, the market towns, the decayed medieval boroughs, the little villages, woods and commons and the cathedral city itself, had been visited. They had not been seen in the full sense, they had been tasted and the appetite whetted. More important than this was the feel of the place, a warmth and an understanding: here was a county where one could live and work and enjoy both, where money and kudos were not the only things, where the rat race did not really matter.

Here, as the years have proved, there is a quality of life which can be enjoyed and lived to the full. It is a warm, kind county.

For 1,500 years Herefordshire has been a Marcher shire, a sort of buffer state, between England, east of the Malverns, and Wales on the west. Part of England and yet in an odd way apart from it, the county has remained one of the most rural in the country. Its natural communications have been north and south along the Wye-Severn trough between the hills. The Romans and the early earls and bishops knew this and both earldom and diocese ran south into north Gloucestershire and Monmouthshire and north into Shropshire, east along the Teme into the western part of Worcestershire and west into the lowlands of Radnorshire and Montgomeryshire. The bishopric still includes most of this today. Even the industrial revolution 50 miles away in the Black Country and around Birmingham did not really affect it.

Unfortunately, the modern administrators did not recognize this and in local government reorganization the county was joined with Worcestershire on the other side of the Malverns, the hills which for so long have been the natural barrier between England and the Marches. The farming community of Herefordshire has been tied administratively to the industrial conurbation in the north-east of the new county.

At the time of the *Domesday Book* the county was divided into 16 hundreds, but in the thirteenth century these were reorganized into 11 which continued until the rural and urban districts were set up in the late nineteenth century. These hundreds were further subdivided into about 230 parishes.

Any agricultural area depends on its market towns and they in turn on the surrounding farming community. Bromyard, Leominster, Kington, Ross-on-Wye and Ledbury in addition to Hereford itself have for some hundreds of years been the main markets of the county. All except Kington were of importance in Saxon times, three of them, Bromyard, Ledbury and Ross having been bishop's manors pre-Conquest. Leominster, like Hereford itself, is based on an important Dark Ages ecclesiastical foundation. None of the five seems to be sited on a prehistoric settlement, but all except Bromyard and Kington have great hill-forts close by which, like Credenhill in the case of Hereford, may have been the site of the earlier town. Of the five only Kington has a medieval castle and only Leominster appears to have had any form of town wall. Today they are, as they have always been, the market centres for much of the county, Hereford itself serving the rich central area, and all now have some industry as well.

In medieval times there were other boroughs and of these Longtown, Pembridge, Wigmore and Weobley are still quite recognizable as small towns with market-places now no longer used as such. Of these Wigmore was a borough at the time of *Domesday Book* as were Clifford, Ewyas Harold and Richard's Castle.

Apart from these one-time boroughs the type of village in the county depends on the methods of land-holding and farming. Big, nucleated villages like Kingsland, Whitbourne and Wellington with farms along a street represent the typical midland village with its open-field system of agriculture. Other parishes like Aymestrey are made up of a series of small townships and in the south-west of the county the big parishes with scattered farms such as Craswall and Michaelchurch Escley are reminiscent of Wales and Cornwall and represent the Celtic system of land-holding.

Very simply the county may be thought of as a red sandstone lowland of rich river valleys surrounded by a ring of hills. These hills are in part older rocks, the Malverns along the eastern fringe being some of the most ancient of the Pre-Cambrian rocks. West and south of them is the Woolhope Dome of Silurian limestone with a similar and closely-related formation in the Aymestrey, Wigmore and Kington area in the north-west. The hills around Bromyard and around Ross are Old Red Sandstone, slightly younger than the Downtonian sandstones of the lowlands, while the south-west is

occupied by the great scarp of the Black Mountains also of Old Red
Sandstone. Much of the red marl of the central and northern
lowland is overlain by glacial drift. The south-eastern lowland with
a considerable thickness of sandstone underlying it weathers down
into a lighter, sandier soil, while in the extreme north-west the
Wigmore basin occupies the bed of a glacial lake. The low,
Downtonian sandstone hills of Wormsley and Dinmore divide the
main lowland area into two parts, one based on Hereford and the
other on Leominster.

There are no deposits of metallic ore in the county and the only
coal is in a Carboniferous outcrop in the extreme south-east. Thus
Herefordshire lacks the mineral resources which form the basis of
industrialization, but weathered, red sandstone has formed a soil of
high fertility and is of great agricultural value.

Hereford cattle are known all over the world and, although the
official date for the beginning of the breed is somewhat later, there
are references to red and white cattle in the sixteenth century. The
improvement in transport and the demand for milk mean that as
well as beef cattle dairy cows are seen in quite considerable numbers
in modern Herefordshire. Sheep and their wool have also been an
important part of the county's farming. Today the Clun and Kerry
breeds are popular, but there are still some flocks of Ryelands, the
local breed, the wool from which was once reckoned to be the best
in England.

However, Herefordshire farming is not all cattle and sheep, for
much of it is good grain-growing country and the existence of
threshing barns over almost the whole of the county shows that it
has been important since at least the sixteenth century. In autumn
a common sight is sacks of apples against the trees in the orchards
awaiting collection, for more cider is made in Hereford than
anywhere else in the world. Hops also are an important crop and
have been since at least the seventeenth century when they are first
mentioned in the inventories which were filed with the wills. A
more recent introduction is sugar-beet which is now an important
crop in the river valleys.

Farming helps to dictate the scenery of the county—grain, hop-yards (not fields), orchards, grazing land and woodland, for timber is an important Herefordshire crop, both softwood and hardwood. The type of farming also decides the shape of the farmyard and its buildings. It is worth looking at a farmhouse and its surroundings rather carefully for a lot can be learnt from such an exploration. Has the barn the big central doors marking a threshing-floor on which flails were used? Has it an octagonal or round building added on one side which contained a horse engine to drive early threshing machines and other farm machinery? Look for the hop-kilns (not oasthouses in Herefordshire) and the granary, both frequently adjoining the house. Look also for the cider-press and mill, the byre with its storage space above, the goosecots where the geese were kept, the pigscots, the cart sheds, the stables and even the laundry. All could be part of a farm organization and today can tell us much about the past.

Throughout history the proximity of Wales has had its influence on the county. Offa built his dyke during the second half of the 8th century and ever since it has marked the line between English and Welsh custom. The area around Hereford was attacked in 760 and, in spite of its strong defences, the city itself was badly damaged in 1055. For the next four centuries a Welsh attack was always likely, Hereford becoming the base for operations against them.

Not all Welsh penetration was warlike. The land of Ewyas in the south-west of the county was in the diocese of St Davids until 1852. Farther down the Monnow is Archenfield, another area of Welsh dedications. Some of the churchyards in these areas remind one of Cornwall and Ireland in their circular shape in prominent positions, a Celtic feature. Many of the smaller Herefordshire churches have the low, plain profile and the small bell turret that so frequently occur in Wales.

It might be thought that the place-names would also show a considerable Welsh influence, but apart from the two areas mentioned above and one or two places in the extreme west near Kington and in the north-west beyond Wigmore they do not. It is clear that the greater part of the county was thoroughly Anglicized in speech and custom in spite of one or two areas where an almost pure Celtic strain seems to have survived in the people with their pale auburn hair, blue eyes and tendency to freckles.

The proximity of the Welsh and the constant fear of attack led to the building of an extraordinary number of castles. Over 90 have been identified in the county, mainly in the west, varying from powerful fortresses like Goodrich and great baronial strongholds like Wigmore, to the much humbler mounds which once carried a wooden tower as at Lingen and Dorstone. Many of these saw their last action during the Civil War of 1642-49, places like Brampton Bryan undergoing quite prolonged sieges, and, with a few exceptions, have been allowed to decay ever since.

For a long time there has been a peaceful penetration as the hill farmers of Radnorshire, Breconshire and Monmouthshire have saved in order to move down on to lowland farms in Herefordshire. This migration still goes on. In spite of this, in Herefordshire as in most rural areas there has been some depopulation over the last 50 years. Housman's plea,

> *stay at home, my lad, and plough*
> *The land . . .*
> *And all about the idle hill*
> *Shepherd your sheep with me,*

is a real one in many a hilly part of the county. In a number of parishes the population is much the same now as in the early eighteenth century, land broken in during the industrial revolution and the two world wars having gone out of use and the houses built at those times having been largely deserted.

The 'travellers' are to be found by the roadside, on quiet lanes and on pieces of common at most times of the year. Today many of them are not true gypsies, but occasionally one still sees the gypsy skirt or overhears a Romany conversation. The writer is assured by gypsies that the 'deep Romany' is rarely heard these days in England,

1. *above* Croft Castle and Church 2. *below* Goodrich Castle above the River Wye

but that what is spoken is a localized, debased form of the language. Some of the old traditions live on and a gypsy funeral is still a sight to be seen and remembered.

Herefordshire villages and towns are places in which to linger. There is little great architecture as far as scale is concerned, but there is some marvellous detail. In the churches two periods stand out, the Norman of the mid-twelfth century and the Decorated of the early fourteenth. The former is famous for the carving of the Herefordshire School of stonemasons. Kilpeck, Shobdon, Rowlstone churches are well-known, but Fownhope, Castle Frome, Brinsop, Stretton Sugwas and Eardisley are other good examples. Many attempts have been made to trace the sources of inspiration of these carvings; Santiago de Compostela in Spain, places in western France and northern Italy have all been suggested. No doubt they had their influence on the style, but above all it must be a flowering of local craftsmanship, the skill which had been used in the carving of the Celtic crosses and which was later to show itself in the beautiful rood-screens of the churches and the overmantels of late Tudor and Stuart houses.

Rather under 200 years later came the outburst of ball-flower ornament, that rich decoration which occurs mainly in a great belt down the western counties and is more common in Herefordshire than in any other district. The south aisle at Leominster, the north chapel at Ledbury and the central tower of the cathedral itself are the great examples, but there are many others all over the county, not all in churches, for it occurs at Brampton Bryan Castle and Broadfield Court.

There are still seven detached church towers in the county and two others were detached when built. Why Hereford and Cornwall should be the counties best known for detached bell-towers seems to be beyond explanation, but it is one of the odd quirks of building history that they are, for between them they have 15 of the 40 in England. A feature of the churchyards is the cross with a niche. Of about 50 known in England and Wales, 37 are in Herefordshire. They seem to have played some part in the Palm Sunday procession

3. The Monnow Valley, Herefordshire's southern boundary

and it has been suggested that the pix was placed in the niche rather than in an Easter Sepulchre in the church itself.

The black-and-white timber-framed houses are the most prominent eye-catchers in the villages and towns. They vary in age from the fourteenth century to the nineteenth and in size from the humblest one-up and one-down cottage to such great houses as Ledbury Park. Some of these are of the cruck type of construction, where two great curved timbers starting from close to the ground meet in an apex at the ridge. Much has been written about its possible Celtic origins, but here it seems to be a development of the late thirteenth, fourteenth and fifteenth centuries to fill a particular need, that of creating a big, open space for the main room of the house, the hall. The walls were constructed separately and then jointed to the main crucks; so that in theory, and sometimes in practice, the walls can be removed and the roof remain in place. It disappeared in domestic buildings when the two-storey house became popular in the sixteenth and seventeenth centuries, but its use continued in farm buildings where plenty of space was required. Bigger and more important are the rare base-cruck houses which were the homes of the rising gentry at the end of the fourteenth and beginning of the fifteenth centuries. An excellent example is the National Trust property at Lower Brockhampton. However, most of the black-and-white houses are the normal box-frame, post and truss type, with a triangular roof dropped on to a timber-framed box, a form of construction found over most of England.

In some parts of the county, particularly in the south-west and parts of the north-west there is a good building stone and in these areas stone houses are the rule. A few of these and a few of the timber-framed are of the long-house type where people and cattle have direct access to each other under the same roof, often using the same front door.

The heavy marls make good, though expensive, brick and as this material became popular so fine examples of its use were built in Herefordshire, not just houses, but farm buildings, dovecotes and even churches.

The earliest traces of settlement in the county have been found in King Arthur's Cave on the Doward, occupied in Paeolithic times, between the Ice Ages. Neolithic and Bronze Age men left their tools and their weapons in a number of places, more substantial remains at Dorstone in the form of a great burial chamber and smaller burial mounds and cists elsewhere.

All over the county there are Iron Age forts crowning the tops of hills. Some of them have been excavated revealing that they were complete, lived-in, little towns, the predecessors of the later market towns and villages. Rather like the ball-flower ornament and the larger cruck buildings a great belt of these hill-forts containing square and rectangular buildings instead of the roughly circular ones of other areas can be followed with Herefordshire one of the prominent counties on it.

The Romans left evidence of three major settlements, *Magnis* (Kenchester) *Ariconium* (Bromsash) and *Bravonium* (Leintwardine) with a number of lesser forts and villas and a road system including the western branch of Watling Street running from *Magnis* west of Hereford to *Viriconium* east of Shrewsbury.

In the fourteenth century William Langland was writing about the Malverns and it seems quite likely that he was born at Longlands near Ledbury. Certainly this early poet owed much of his influence to Herefordshire and others have found the same inspiration in the centuries which have passed since his day. Thomas Traherne, whose work has recently been recognized as being among the great metaphysical poetry of the seventeenth century was born in Hereford, while in this century the late poet laureate, John Masefield, was a Ledbury boy. Elizabeth Barratt Browning spent her girlhood at Cradley and Wordsworth also knew the county well, having stayed with friends in different parts of Herefordshire.

Apart from Langland two other early pieces of literature have connections with the county. The *Ancrene Wisse* dates from the early thirteenth century and was at one time in the possession of St James Church at Wigmore. It seems possible that it was advice to the anchorites or nuns of Deerfold, or to the then recently founded nunnery at Limebrook. It is now in the library of Corpus Christi College, Cambridge. The other is the fourteenth-century *Red Book of Hergest* which is almost a library in itself and contains the *Mabinogion,* a great collection of early Welsh history and legend inextricably mixed.

Some of the dialect words in parts of the county are as old as these works or even older. Langland would no doubt have recognized 'costrel' (a wooden bottle) and 'yauling' (howling) while 'arg' (argue) and 'slang' (long, narrow strip of land) have their origins in Norman French. The differences in dialect between areas quite close to each other is noticeable; even within the catchment area of one Herefordshire rural secondary school there can be quite distinct dialects.

A county of often remote settlements is bound to have its old customs and its folklore. Some of it is part of a national theme, some limited to the county and some intensely local. The barbarous practice of cock fighting continued very late in Herefordshire and even in the last decade the writer has seen game cocks kept in an isolated farm building. In an area so dependent on the land and its produce harvest is bound to play an important part in the round of the year, the harvest home still being one of the highlights of the calendar in some parts of the county. As in many parts of the country there are stories of secret tunnels, some of them so obviously impossible that it seems strange that the belief in them even existed, stranger still that such belief still continues. Most of them can be explained away as drainage tunnels.

In a county of numerous hedgerows wild flowers are certain to be plentiful. Woods full of bluebells and wood anemone in spring, primroses in the hedges and cowslips on the banks, and snowdrops early in the year are a common sight. However, some parts have their own special flora. The Doward with its Carboniferous limestone and the Silurian areas are good examples. Orchids are relatively plentiful, as is the autumn crocus and, on the Dorward, the limeloving green and stinking hellebores, bloody cranesbill and madder are found. The higher, sub-alpine area of the Black Mountains with its almost entirely sandstone rock provides a contrast with the other parts of the county, being of considerable interest to the botanist. It is interesting to note the occurrence of some rather rare plants near the sites of some of the old religious houses: henbane at Wigmore, thorn apple near Dinmore, asarabacca near Limebrook, and danewort and elecampane near Aconbury.

There is a considerable variety of ferns found in the county and examples of well over half the known species of British mosses occur. Again the limestone areas, and especially the Doward, are those with most interest for the botanist. In its early days the county society, the Woolhope Club, carried out a series of very successful fungus forays and the British Mycological Society traces its ancestry back to that body. Between 1,400 and 1,500 species of fungi have been found in the county. It is not everybody's idea of the way to spend a day, but clearly it has given much pleasure to quite a number of people over the past 125 years.

It is said that if nature was left to its own devices for 300 years Herefordshire would be largely covered by oak woods. Today much of the woodland is coniferous, but by no means all of it, and some fine examples of hardwoods occur in the county and are still being planted. The lime-loving beech is found at its best on the Carboniferous limestone in the south, where the rowan, large and small-leaved limes, dogwood and field maple occur and it was also in this area that the writer saw a rare example of the black poplar. The holly is found in hedgerows all over the county. Some fine parkland oaks can be seen at Brampton Bryan, Moccas and Garnons, while at the latter are some magnificent plantations of oak. Today the elm is suffering badly and its disappearance is going to make a difference to the Herefordshire scene. The ash, the sycamore, the alder and the willow grow well, the last named being popular in the river valleys. Perhaps as a warning to those who decide to walk through the county's woodlands it should be pointed out that 72 species of bramble have been recorded.

It is perhaps best not to say too much about birds as there are so many, and they are so interesting to watch. Watching is surely the thing to do, not necessarily with binoculars and wearing gumboots, but just through the window, or sitting quietly at the edge of a wood or down by the river. Today, hardly noticing them, the writer has seen through his window four species of tit, three species of finch, the hedge sparrow and the house sparrow, a jay, wood pigeon and collared doves, thrushes, blackbirds, robins, jackdaws, starlings, wren and a kestrel. Often there would have been a wagtail, a woodpecker and a nuthatch. In summer there will be other species; on many a morning a goldcrest works the rockery outside the kitchen window and presently the owl will be calling in the churchyard next door. A few hundred yards down the road a buzzard has his favourite perch and there are coots, swans, pheasants and partridges. The thrill of finding a goldcrest's nest, of hearing a corncrake on a summer evening and of watching a hen partridge march her chicks along a road; this is all part of the joy of this county.

Across the valley is Mortimer Forest. Here is the home of that rarity, the dark, long-haired fallow deer, a variant of the common British fallow. Badgers, foxes and grey squirrels are seen comparatively frequently. The red squirrel is still to be found in a few parts of the county. A few years ago on the main Leominster-Hereford road a weasel dragged his prey to the white line, waited there until the traffic had passed and then proceeded across the road. The most thrilling sight was a stoat in ermine early in 1964; perhaps he was expecting a repeat of the previous winter. Weasels and stoats, like rabbits and hares, are not uncommon sights. Another animal which has been re-establishing itself over the past few years is the polecat. Again it is a matter of watching, of going around with eyes and ears open. These animals and the smaller rodents are about and are there to be seen. A rare sight is the otter, but there was sure evidence of one last summer when on the banks of the Lugg was a partly-eaten salmon. Clearly there are some around, but not many. The hedgehog is perhaps getting a little more used to the car, and moles and shrews seem plentiful enough.

Fox-hunting and otter-hunting provide a colourful spectacle at certain times of the year. Opinions may differ over hunting, but nobody can deny the colour and the nostalgic appeal particularly of a fox-hunting meet with the ceremony of the stirrup-cup, the master, the huntsman and the horn.

Because most, not quite all, roads lead to Hereford the earlier chapters of the book will follow the river valleys into the city and the migration down them from Wales. Later chapters will deal with the south-west and the north-west where Hereford itself is rather more remote, where sometimes trade looks to market towns just across the border with other counties, and where in medieval times the great Marcher barons held sway.

ONE

Ross and the Southern Wye

The present-day traveller coming to Herefordshire by road is likely to come off the motorway at Ross-on-Wye. If he comes into the town he will approach it up a steep hill with what appears to be a medieval defensive tower and a town wall at the top. In fact, although well weathered, they date from the late 1830s when Ross was 'gothicized'.

The town became a fashionable resort for a time with the Royal Hotel built on the site of the old bishop's palace and a number of other good late Georgian and Regency hotels and houses. The wall and the tower, the lock-up in New Street, the folly in a garden in Edde Cross Street and numerous other bits of gothic red sandstone date from the 1830s and 1840s, the town's contribution to the Romantic Revival. What would Jane Austen have written about it?

A century and a half earlier Ross had been the home of John Kyrle, 1637—1724, the 'Man of Ross', and today his influence and generosity still have their effect on the town. At this distance in time it is difficult to get an accurate picture of the man, in spite of Pope's poem, but he was very popular and apparently cheerful and renowned for his fair-mindedness. His house still stands opposite the Town Hall. It is a good example of seventeenth-century timber-framing while in the garden behind is a red sandstone summerhouse; if this was built by John Kyrle it is a very early example. Kyrle gave a piece of land west of the church to the town. It is known as the

Prospect and any walk around Ross can well start from there. From it one looks over a long meander of the Wye across the bridge of the dual carriageway to the hills away to the north or westwards over Wilton Bridge and the ruined castle. At any time of the year it is a view which should not be missed.

Not only John Kyrle gave money to help his fellow citizens in Ross, for there are three sets of almshouses of which the most obvious are those given by William Rudhall in 1575, across the road from the east end of the churchyard. They are of red sandstone with mullioned windows and look their best in the light of the evening sun.

The church itself, set high above the town is of quite considerable interest. Of special note are the tombs of William and Ann Rudhall, 1530, and John and Mary Rudhall, 1636. These are both alabaster altar tombs, the latter having a black marble top. The east window is of fifteenth-century glass probably from the bishop's palace at Stretton Sugwas. The two outer lights are of Hereford's two saints, St Ethelbert and St Thomas Cantilupe, while the inner lights show St Ann and the Virgin and St Joachim. Inside the east window of the north aisle are two elm trees growing. A sad reminder of past days is the churchyard cross commemorating 315 parishioners who died of plague in 1637.

Back in the market-place is the market-hall built between 1660 and 1674. Unlike the other Herefordshire examples it is of red sandstone, not timber-framed, but is built on the normal pattern of an open, arcaded ground floor and a hall above. From here the triangular-shaped market-place falls away steeply down the hill to become Broad Street. Until the last century a row of timber-framed houses known as Under-Hell ran from the hall down the street dividing it into two. Ledbury and Hereford had similar rows in the market-place.

Ross is still a holiday resort as the planners of the early Victorian era wished it to be, but it is also a market town as it has been since the days when the bishops of Hereford established a market *c.* 1120 and a borough some 30 years later. By 1285 the bishop had 105 tenants in Ross. Come into Ross on market day and see just how busy a centre for the surrounding agricultural area it is. Above the modern shop fronts the timber-framing of earlier buildings is to be seen, a look up some of the alleyways shows that many of the old houses and shops still survive behind more recent brick or stone or plastered fronts.

At the bottom of Broad Street is Brookend Street where by the stream is the heart of the old industrial area of Ross, the water-mill. Also here is the Railway Inn, a pleasant building of the early eighteenth century with a good mid-nineteenth century public house front, a comparatively rare sight today.

Ross has grown because of its position on the river. An ancient ford existed at Wilton; a castle, now in ruins, was built to protect it, and the town was founded on the opposite bank. Leland in the sixteenth century mentions the 'wood bridge by Roose' which may have been at the bottom of Wye Street where a ferry ran later. In 1599 a stone bridge was built at Wilton and has been the main access to Ross from the north ever since, except for a short period during the Civil War when one arch at the Hereford end was destroyed as a defensive measure.

In 1770 the Rev. William Gilpin took a boat down the Wye as a result of which in 1782 he published *Observations on the River Wye*. Thomas Gray and Samuel Ireland also wrote about the Wye and its natural beauty. The cult of the Picturesque expounded by Uvedale Price and Richard Payne Knight was to have a considerable effect on Ross and the Wye below it. By the end of the century there were eight boats prepared to take the wealthy to Monmouth for one and a half guineas or to Chepstow for three guineas. In 1799 Charles Heath brought out the first edition of his *Excursion down the Wye*. The Wye tourist industry had been born. Many books were to follow; the river seems to draw people to it to describe its beauties.

The cult of the Picturesque affected not only Ross but the Goodrich area to the south. Here is the best preserved castle in the county in a magnificent situation overlooking the Wye. It is a building full of fascinating glimpses, not only of the river, but of detail in the various parts of the castle, the arches of the great hall, the fireplace hoods, the chapel, the great square keep itself and the high, fin-like buttresses of the corner towers. Half a mile away overlooking Kerne Bridge are the ruins of Flanesford Priory, an Augustinian house founded in 1346.

With these two truly picturesque, beautifully situated ruins so close by perhaps it is not surprising that in 1828 was begun Goodrich Court a vast and fantastic turreted and castellated building only half a mile from the castle. For 120 years it dominated the scene, looking down over the Wye, romantic, Rhinelike, a symbol of early nineteenth-century wealth and thought. Blore must have had legend and the early medieval period in mind when he designed it for Sir Samuel Rush Meyrick who used it to house his extensive collection of medieval armour. Wordsworth called it an 'impertinent structure' and wished for the power to blow it away.

Now all is gone except the eastern gatehouse on the dual carriageway from Ross to Monmouth. Red sandstone, round gate towers with conical roofs and machicolation give us an idea of the appearance of the main building, now only preserved in photographs and romantic drawings making this part of the Wye look like the Rhine Gorge. Goodrich village itself has its share of romantic building, the Olde Hostelrie with its tall windows and pinnacles and Y Crwys being the most likely to catch the eye. Perhaps the Romantic architecture of Ross received its inspiration from here.

Not that this type of building was new to the county. Smirke had begun Eastnor Castle in 1812, Downton had been built between 1772 and 1778, Bollitree about the same time, and Croft Castle had been given a gothick front even earlier than this and as early as 1753 Shobdon Church had been rebuilt in the Strawberry Hill Gothic style. Thus Ross comes at the end of a line of romantic buildings in Herefordshire.

In Goodrich Church is preserved a chalice given by Dean Swift whose grandfather had been the staunchly loyal Royalist vicar here during the Civil War.

Many of the Ross tourists found their way to the Doward and Symonds Yat and still do. The latter is justly famous for its view of the limestone gorge, the Seven Sisters rock and the great loop of the Wye. Perhaps some feel it is spoiled by visitors and the attempt to cater for them, yet these are minor intrusions into such a scene as this. It is too grand, too peaceful to be really damaged by this type of business venture.

From here are overlooked the tree-lined slopes of the Dowards, Great and Little. On the latter is King Arthur's Cave. This late Celtic leader gets blamed for many things and his name occurs twice at least in the county. Stone Age man lived in this cave and his remains and those of his prey have been found in excavations here. To the naturalist this area is a treasure trove, some 700 species of flora and nearly 300 mosses and liverworts having been recorded here.

It was in this area that Slippery Jimmy lived in a much later man-made den some four feet in diameter and seven or eight feet high. He was a victim of enclosure evictions in the 1830s and lived as a hermit in this thickly thatched home for almost 40 years, living off what he could trap and grow. The site of his cave has since been destroyed by quarrying.

A completely different aspect is to be found in the area south of the town; this is Herefordshire's coal-mining area. Not that there has ever been a black, industrial revolution belt here, but, nevertheless, open-cast coal mining on a small scale still goes on here on the edge of the Forest of Dean coalfield. The coal is close to the surface in a bed only a few feet thick and as a field is stripped of its coal it is brought back to use as farmland and within two years is bearing grain again. Yet this industrial use has given rise on these hills to a no-man's-land of narrow, often unsurfaced lanes, a real maze, with little houses built by the miners of 150 and 200 years ago. Nevertheless, in the midst of this area where the feeling is of the industrial revolution there are glimpses of an older past.

In the valley are Hill Court and Old Hill Court. The latter is a good, timber-framed, early sixteenth-century house. Down a half-mile-long avenue it faces its brick successor built in the last two years of the seventeenth century. Much added to about 25 years later the latter's warm-coloured bricks made from the local clay fit happily into this landscape from which they came.

On the hill out from Walford is the tastefully restored timber-framed house of Upper Wythall, typical of the period about 1600 and further up again on a steep slope just before the top is another, smaller black-and-white house with opposite it a black poplar. It is a fine, beautiful tree of a type rarely found today, the old, native poplar common before the strangers from Lombardy were introduced. In shape it is not unlike the oak and indeed it was one of the trees used to provide timber for cruck buildings.

Moving eastwards on the very edge of the county is Euroclydon, a nineteenth-century industrialist's house with its own private and very early gas works, now little more than a mound in a field. There were several of these enterprising landowners in the county who in the days before public gas supplies and private electricity generators had their own gas works to light the 'big house'. It is noticeable that they are sited well away from the houses; a very sensible and necessary precaution.

There is evidence of much earlier industry in the woods to the north. The observant walker will notice an occasional levelled area in the side of the hill. Frequently when the grass is cleared from it the soil will be found to be mainly charcoal, the levelled-out area being the site of charcoal burning. On the tops of some of these hills the archaeologists can point out signs of Roman iron working.

The local centre 1,800 years ago was *Ariconium,* close to the modern cross-roads at Bromsash, some four miles east of Ross. It appears to have been a small Roman town, a meeting place of their roads and probably the centre for the local iron industry.

This same metal had its importance hundreds of years later and there are remains of forges just off the dual carriageway west of Ross near Goodrich and at St Weonards further west again where a farm bears the name, Old Furnace. Today it is not easy to imagine these sixteenth and seventeenth-century ironworks, but small though they were by modern standards they were important little industrial sites in their day as will be seen when Downton in the north of the county is reached. 'Roaring Meg' a mortar on the Castle Green at

Hereford was cast locally and used in the capture of Goodrich Castle in 1646.

Between this area of past iron working and Ross are the parishes of Hope Mansell and Weston-under-Penyard. Their churches are two of a little group with quite early roofs of a type more typical of the English midlands than the Marches, trussed rafters with scissors braces, and no longitudinal strengthening at all, both probably dating from the fourteenth century. Hope Mansell is hidden away in a remote valley, secluded, sheltered, white with blossom in spring and tinged with the red and brown of leaves after the early autumn frosts.

Between it and Weston is the hamlet of Ryeford with its Baptist Chapel of 1662 now doing duty as a Sunday school and almost hidden by its successor. These small, early non-conformist places of worship which are to be found in several Herefordshire villages are worth looking at not only in admiration of the way in which their builders were determined to have somewhere to hold their services, but also as examples of the simple, practical way in which they are constructed. Often there is much beauty in their simplicity.

Weston is certainly not hidden, standing on the main Ross–Gloucester road overlooked by its church on the hill. Yet the best of it is not quite so obvious. In spite of the timber-framed house facing the church porch it is a stone village in which the local red sandstone has been used. Up on Penyard are the scanty remains of a stone castle while to the north of the village are Bollitree and the old rectory, both fine, late seventeenth-century houses. At Bollitree the north and east fronts and the barn were given gothick towers, doorways and windows probably about 1775 and certainly before 1789. What cannot be seen from outside, however, is that this romantic exterior hides a much earlier timber-framed structure. Facing it across the moat-cum-duck-pond is an enclosed garden with a modern house inside. The brick garden wall is probably contemporary with the late seventeenth-century main house of Bollitree and over the doorway are the arms of the Merrick family who lived here and also at Street, down the hill towards the village. This is another house to be quietly admired from the road across its pleasant garden with the datestone above the doorway with the initials I and E M and the date 1711.

These houses and the earlier Weston House by the main road to the west of the village show the wealth of this parish, derived from its farming.

North of Ross beyond the view from the Prospect the river is less well known, more inaccessible, more intimate. The great landowners throughout the centuries, however, have appreciated the wealth and shelter of the valley and the beauty of the river. Along the valley from Ross to Hereford are houses of varying dates, most of them not so much mansions as fine homes of wealthy yeomen, men often armigerous, playing their part locally and sometimes nationally, but who would describe themselves as farmers as well as gentlemen.

The best way to see the Wye is probably to travel down it by canoe, but for those with less time and energy there are minor roads running close to the river through delightful scenery. One from Ross goes down the Hill of Eaton, through Hole-in-the-Wall down to Fawley and Brockhampton to Fownhope. It is a road to linger on, at times going across good, open farmland, at others squeezed between the woods and the river.

At Brampton Abbotts the church contains a brass to John Rudhall, 1506, other members of whose family were commemorated at Ross. At the corner of the small parish is the beautifully situated Rudhall House, with work from every century from the fourteenth to the present. Here the Chelsea Pensioners found a home during the Second World War.

At How Caple Court and church lie next to each other, but down in the valley below is the main part of the village with its mill and two gardens with chinoiserie summerhouses, an unexpected nineteenth-century conceit in this very rural bit of Herefordshire.

King's Caple is situated almost at the end of one of the great meanders of the river, but on the way is Fawley Court. The west front of red sandstone, with mullioned and transomed windows looks out over its well-kept garden, but behind is an equally fine timber-framed section looking east. Here lived the Kyrle family in the seventeenth century, and the house seems to have been built mainly by them. With its duck pond, trees, garden and barns it forms a grouping not easily forgotten. The little Norman chapel of Fawley is a mile away right by the river.

At King's Caple Church the early fourteenth-century ball-flower ornament occurs, but the church will be remembered for the seventeenth-century panelled pulpit with its sounding board and the stone-vaulted roofs of the porch and the Aramstone Chapel. Unfortunately the Georgian house of the family which gave its name to the chapel has been demolished.

The road runs close to the river to Brockhampton. Much of the way there is woodland between it and the Wye, but there are some beautiful glimpses through the trees. Brockhampton, neat and tidy, a one-time estate village, contains a surprise, a church built in 1902 and one of the most impressive 'of its date in any country'. W. R. Lethaby, the architect, was a follower of William Morris, an Arts-and-Crafts man. At Brockhampton he used concrete for the steep pointed tunnel-vaulting giving an impression which is more common in the churches of 20 years later. The roof is thatched. Tapestries in the church were designed by Burne-Jones and made at William Morris's workshops. The old church, now roofless, is in the grounds of the Court, now a hotel.

At Fownhope the minor road rejoins a rather more important one from Ross to Hereford, the village having grown along this in a form of ribbon development. Unlike the area to the east of it Fownhope is a timber-framed village with black-and-white houses along both sides of the main road. In the late eighteenth and the nineteenth centuries brick was the fashionable material and a fascinating example of changing tastes can be seen in the front of the Green Man Inn. Looked at from the entry into the courtyard it can be seen that the original timber-framed wall was given a brick face, probably early in the last century, and now this in its turn has been refaced in timber-framing. This was done in 1965, making a kind of sandwich with brick in the middle.

4.   The Wye Valley from Symonds Yat

An old custom still continues in Fownhope on Oak-apple Day when the Hearts of Oak Society walk through the village, each member carrying a club decorated with flowers, the procession finishing at the Green Man, no doubt to celebrate Prince Charles' escape 300 years ago.

In the church the tympanum of one of the Norman doorways has been reset. It is a typical piece of carving of the Herefordshire School of the twelfth century of the Virgin and Child both with their hands raised in blessing and is very well preserved. Outside the church is the village stocks, across the road is a fine threshing barn, and, on the corner by the church, a milestone, probably from turnpike days, giving the exact distance in miles and yards to Ross and Hereford.

Beyond Fownhope the road runs close to the river, the Woolhope Hills coming right down to the bank and leaving little room for it. Just south of Mordiford is a bridge across the Wye. During the Second World War the Home Guard watched over it from a spot above the road ready to fire, if the need arose, what appears to have been a latter-day version of Roaring Meg. If it had ever had to be used there may well have been casualties among those who fired it as well as the intended victims. Just above the bridge are the very slight remains of a quay where river barges used to load and unload in the days when they plied their trade from Chepstow to Hereford.

On the western side of the river is a maze of lanes between the Wye and the main road south. Except close to the river on the flood plain it is broken country, much of it wooded, and from the hills there are fine views to the Malverns, to Ross and May Hill and, as one gets farther south, to the Black Mountains. Before the climb up begins there is a group of villages on this rich farming land close to the river. It is no accident that the College of Agriculture is situated here close to Holme Lacy where is also one of the county's greatest mansions, once the home of the Scudamores, now a hospital. The house was built *c.* 1675-80 and is a very advanced design for its time but very restrained. The interior has a series of magnificent plaster ceilings of 1680-90 but its beautiful Grinling Gibbons garlands and trophies have gone to New York and to Kentchurch Court.

5. *above* Arthur's Stone, a Neolithic chambered tomb on Merbach Hill;
6. *below* Britain's biggest chained library, Hereford Cathedral

The Scudamores succeeded the de Lacys here in the fourteenth century and remained until this branch died out in 1820. Their fine tombs still remain in the church a mile away from the little village green and the great house. Foremost among them are the altar tomb with alabaster effigies of John Scudamore, 1571, and Sibell his wife who was a Vaughan of Hergest; of James Scudamore, 1668, in marble and his wife Jane, 1700. Changing customs are shown in the fact that the last of these has no effigy, but is simply an elaborate wall monument.

North of Holme Lacy rises Dinedor or Oyster Hill with a big, Iron Age hill-fort at the top, perhaps one of the predecessors of Hereford itself. Beneath, now in the care of the Department of the Environment and lying on the flat land close to the river is Rotherwas Chapel with its late sixteenth-century hammerbeam roof. The great house to which it belonged no longer survives though some of its panelling and one of its fireplaces are now in Massachusetts.

In a peaceful valley among the hills Margery, wife of William de Ley, founded a priory of Augustinian nuns at Aconbury early in the thirteenth century. Their church still stands, though now redundant. Those who brave the nettles and briars of the churchyard can still find some trace of the cloisters on the south side. It is strange to imagine the pomp and beauty which this quiet, little hamlet must have seen in the 300 years before the Dissolution.

Another great hill-fort, Aconbury, is situated high up in the woods above the nunnery.

Hoarwithy is one of those places where a stranger has almost to shake himself to make sure he is not in Italy, for high up on the hill above the river is St Catherine's Church, which in its present state dates from the 1880s. It is a remarkable piece of Italian and semi-Byzantine architecture. The architect was J. P. Seddon and his inspiration must have been purely south Italian. Perhaps the most impressive sight is as one clambers up the path and through the open base of the campanile sees arch following arch along the cloister, while inside the good contemporary stained glass, the cosmati work of the ambo which takes the place of a pulpit and the grey Devon marble of the great columns carrying the cupola all provide memories to take away of this most unexpected building. The work was paid for by the then vicar, the Rev. William Poole.

Hoarwithy is at the western end of a crossing of the Wye where for many years there was a ferry to King's Caple and Fawley, but this was replaced by an iron bridge about 1880. The boatman's high, narrow house by the river became the toll-house for the bridge and, though no longer used for this purpose, is still lived in. Today the village is something of a minor holiday resort with caravans in the fields by the river and canoes on it.

The road to Ross has some beautiful views along this stretch of the river. Those with time can follow a road which leads to Sellack and Foy, hamlets on a tongue formed by a long meander of the river. Each is a small cluster of houses round its church and, in the case of Sellack, a second at the court, Caradoc Court, a fine sixteenth and seventeenth-century house, partly stone, partly timber-framed. This mixture in a sense reflects the houses all the way along this western side of the river from Hereford to Ross, some stone, some black-and-white timber-framed, some a bit of both. In 1640 John Abrahall left money to have made 'a fayer window contayning three lights and there place the same after the same manner as such a window is placed in the church of Sellack'. Thus here there is a Perpendicular window with its stained glass all deliberately copied *c.* 1675.

On the main road is Peterstow with its little village green and just off is Bridstow, the traffic and the dual carriageway warning the traveller that he is back close to Ross again.

The area to the west of the Wye and between the Worm Brook and the Monnow in this southern part of the county was known as Archenfield. Here Welsh custom prevailed for 200 years or more after the Norman conquest. The men of this area had the doubtful privilege of forming the vanguard of the English army against the Welsh and on the return, the rearguard. Presumably there was some animosity between them and their kinsfolk. Today in the deanery of Archenfield many of the churches are dedicated to Welsh saints. One of the customs which continued here was that of gavelkind, a system of inheritance by which a man's property is shared equally among his offspring. Another, which lasted up to 1911, was that of having the right of free fishing in the Wye in the area south of Holme Lacy.

West of the main Hereford–Ross road the names and dedications are Celtic and the villages remind one of Wales or Cornwall.

The names Welsh Bicknor and Welsh Newton are reminders of earlier days. In the former parish is Courtfield, now occupied by the Mill Hill Fathers founded by Cardinal Vaughan to train young men for missionary work. For 300 years Courtfield was the home of the Vaughans though the present house dates mainly from 1805. It is in a magnificent position overlooking the river and it was here in the last century that Colonel Francis John Vaughan and his wife Louisa Elizabeth had 13 children, six of whom became priests and four nuns. It was Herbert, one of the sons, who became Cardinal Vaughan.

At Whitchurch on the way to Symonds Yat is Old Court. Built of stone with mullioned and transomed windows, it looks at first sight like a Cornish or Devon house of the sixteenth century. Inside, local craft traditions appear in the timber-framed partition between passage and hall and hall and wing and in the finely moulded beams of the ceiling. In this house both the stonemason and the carpenter could show their skills. The church is dedicated to St Dubricius, a local saint of whom more will be written later.

Whitchurch is the last of the Herefordshire villages on the banks of the Wye and the other settlements in Archenfield are in much hillier country.

Welsh Newton is on the main Monmouth to Hereford road at a spot where the valley opens out just a little and the village is clustered round its small church. This has, very surprisingly, a stone screen between nave and chancel with the ball-flower ornament of the early fourteenth century as decoration. A chantry was founded in the church as late as 1547 when moves were already afoot to confiscate the wealth of chantries; was it the last to be founded in England? In the churchyard is a slab to 'I. K. Dyed the 22 August

Anno Do 1679'; this is John Kemble who was martyred in that year and of whom more will be found elsewhere in this book.

Llangarron village is on a hillside around a roughly circular churchyard, typical of the Celtic fringe of Britain. The church is dedicated to St Deinst, whose only other church is Itton in Monmouthshire. The lanes leading to the village run between good farmland, the wealth of which no doubt paid for the fine farmhouses at Langstone, Bernithon, Treribble, Ruxton and The Grove. The first three all date from the late seventeenth century, Langstone being a particularly fine example; like Bernithon, it is built of brick. Deep in a valley is Trereece Mill still with its wheel, and along the stream still stands the pump-house of the Llangarron water supply built in 1906 which augmented the earlier system of 1888. The story of its installation is a real saga of late nineteenth-century local government.

Perhaps the heart of Archenfield could be thought of as Hentland, for here in the fifth century St Dubricius himself founded a college for priests. He was probably born at Madley and his college at Hentland is said to have attracted over 2,000 clerics in the seven years before he moved it to Moccas. Today Hentland is almost forgotten, a church and one or two cottages. The dedication is to St Dubricius and, whilst nothing remains from the Dark Ages, there is a fine churchyard cross and in the church part of the screen is original fifteenth-century work.

Hentland, Sellack and King's Caple across the river are three Herefordshire parishes where on Palm Sunday Pax cakes, little, flat cakes with the Agnus Dei on them, are distributed after morning service. The blessing that goes with them, 'Peace and Good Neighbourhood', is meant to bring peace to any who are quarrelling. They are the result of a sixteenth-century Scudamore bequest.

The motorist on the main Hereford to Ross road may just glimpse the church of St Dinabo at Llandinabo with its partly timber-framed, partly stone house adjoining. They form a picturesque group, but in the church is one of the memorable screens of Herefordshire. Beautifully carved with its frieze of dolphins, angels, and a mermaid, it also shows some early Renaissance influences. It probably dates from the period just before Henry VIII's Reformation, some time perhaps in the late 1620s. Dating from 100 years later, 1629, is a brass to a boy, Thomas Tompkins, who was drowned. It is on the north wall of the chancel and shows him, wearing a collar with a pendant cross, half-submerged in a pool of water.

Not really in Archenfield but, nevertheless in the Wye valley between Ross and Hereford, are Dewsall and Callow. The former at the end of a long lane is another of the big house and church groups. Dewsall Court shows a feature found elsewhere in the county, a wing, balancing the parlour wing, but not, as would be expected, a service wing. It is entirely used for farm purposes except for the kitchen on the ground floor. The church is a plain rectangle with a tiny bell turret, one of several in Herefordshire which is reminiscent of Wales. Set in the shelter of the hill and trees at the end of the valley it could well be part of Radnorshire or Breconshire.

Callow has a very unusual ghost, a house not a person. On the first edition of the Ordance Survey Map the main road south from Hereford is shown going up the hill through Callow. In those days there was a coaching inn in the village and across the fields farther up the hill was a house. Occasionally a passenger would change his mind and would not be on the coach next morning. But had he indeed done so? Eventually the secret was out, the passengers had ended their journey in Callow in the house across the fields. The house was allowed to decay, fall down, yet occasionally, unable to free itself from its past evils, the ghost house is seen on the old site.

Back in Archenfield just south of Dewsall is Llanwarne, in the valley of the Gamber, a little tributary of the Wye. It is beautifully situated with its ruinous, medieval church and close by its smart nineteenth-century replacement. Downstream, on higher land east of the river are Pencoyd and Michaelchurch, with typical small churches. The latter, however, still contains much of its thir-teenth-century painted decoration on the plaster of the walls. Even more surprising is a stoup which on examination proves to be a

Roman altar. Tretire lies down in the valley, but on the western side making no attempt to hide itself is St Weonards. The dedication is unique in England. The glory of the church is the early sixteenth-century stained glass window in the north chapel. One of the saints shown is St Weonard, wearing olive green and holding a book and an axe. One inscription in the window asks for prayers for the soul of Richard Minors, 1521. There was a John de Mynors probably living at Treago in the early fourteenth century and the family are still there in the castle half a mile from the church. This is a square building with round angle towers and, although some of the stonework may go back to earlier periods, the main construction seems to be late fifteenth- and early sixteenth-century.

'Orcop, God help us', was a Herefordshire saying of the last century. It is rather cut off and it is easy to imagine the help of the Almighty being needed to get out of the village in bad weather. Actually, the 'God help us' is more probably a corruption of the 'Ora pro nobis' inscribed on the bells in the church which stands there on its hill surrounded by a ring of higher hills, with the motte and bailey of the castle a few hundred yards away. On a fine summer day there is peace and quiet here and it is difficult to imagine the noise of the main roads only four miles to the east and west. A road runs along the southern face of Orcop Hill following the 800 feet contour. From there the view extends from the Black Mountains in the west to the Forest of Dean in the east. Climb to the top, and look north-east to the great hill-forts of Aconbury and Dinedor, east to Caplar and south to Little Doward. It is from a viewpoint like this that one can appreciate the siting of these Iron Age fortifications on the strategic points of this ring of hills around this part of the Wye.

Perhaps this is the place to finish this chapter and sit and contemplate on the peaceful view, on the scenery of the Wye, its natural beauty and its man-made 'romantic' buildings, the barges of the traders, the coracles of the fishermen and the canoes and anglers of the present age.

TWO

The Valley
of the Frome

The Frome is the least of the county's rivers, rising in the hills on the north-eastern edge of Herefordshire in an area of small villages and scattered farmsteads, much of which was common land until the early years of the last century. It has a character all of its own and the only way to see some of it and enjoy it to the full is on foot.

From Three Gates on the Bromyard-Stourport road a gated road runs across the fields to the west to Wolferlow, just a tiny hamlet with a church, and on beyond until suddenly it comes out on the edge of the escarpment looking across the valley to Stoke Bliss and Collington. It is a view which is perhaps at its very best early on a summer morning, but it is also a lovely spot from which to watch the sun set.

While in this corner of the county it is worthwhile moving away from the Frome valley to look at the Sapey Brook area to the east. For a time, between Upper Sapey in Herefordshire and Lower in Worcestershire, the brook marks the boundary. There is a beautiful, even though slightly precarious, walk along the bank where it is possible to see tufa (travertine) still being deposited on the river cliffs. This stone was used for windows and doorways by some of the Norman builders. A footpath leads up from the river past Winsley Farm and Tipton Hall to Tedstone Delamere. Both these houses have quite elaborate hopkilns which show clearly how methods have changed over the last three centuries. Tipton is a fine late medieval house with a hall and two cross-wings much altered in the seventeenth and eighteenth centuries.

For the motorist there is a perfectly good road from Upper Sapey or Wolferlow to Tedstone Delamere where the little church lies alone in a field surrounded by the house platforms and sunken ways of a now disappeared medieval village. Some of the church walling may be pre-Conquest for there is a triangular strip label in the blocked north doorway. Here also tufa is used in two of the windows and the quoins at the west end, but the treasure is the fourteenth-century churchyard cross with its crucifix on one side and the Virgin and Child on the other. Up the hill from the church is the hall surrounded by its ditch or 'ha-ha' to keep out the sheep.

The road goes on from the little village down into the valley of the Sapey Brook across Badley Wood Common with its collection of small, late, timber-framed houses to the much bigger settlement of Whitbourne, the centre of a large parish and one-time manor of the bishops of Hereford. The church has a fine Norman font with a rather crude Agnus Dei on it, the lamb looking more like a donkey, and star-shaped decoration. The south doorway is also Norman, the outer ornament being obvious, but a look at the inside reveals a head and a leaf stop on the chamfer of the jambs. However, the most unusual thing in the church is a late fifteenth-century cope of red velvet embroidered with the Assumption. It was quite probably the property of one of the bishops whose medieval, moated palace still stands just south-east of the church. The house was enlarged in the seventeenth century by the great Parliamentary leader, Colonel Birch, and then again in the nineteenth. Inside, the original medieval roof is still intact. In 1633 was buried in the church Bishop Francis Godwin whose book *The Man in the Moon* could be thought of as an early attempt at science fiction, though he is better known for his more scholarly work on English bishops.

In the village are some houses of cruck construction, but the chimneys on a house just over 100 yards west of the church are even rarer, especially in this area. They are of sixteenth-century brick, one with zigzag ornament and the other with big, rounded pellets, an unusual form of chimney decoration. The village has good examples of houses both black-and-white, timber-framed and brick. A delightfully peaceful lane through beautiful scenery leads almost due north out of the village up the Tedney valley.

In the opposite direction between the village and the main Worcester-Bromyard road is Whitborne Hall, built in 1861-62 on the model of the Erechtheum with a massive Ionic portico. It can be seen from the main road, but a closer view may be obtained from a gated road through fields and woods leading to Sandy Cross on the Bromyard-Stourport road, which would be worth following even if the hall were not there. However, the lovely little north lodge on the road from Tedstone Delamere is in some ways the best building of the Whitbourne Hall estate.

Across the main road a lane leads southwards to the other part of the parish. Here one sees the mixture of building styles and materials which occurs so often in the county. On the right across an orchard is Huntlands, timber-framed of cruck construction, while on the east is Old Gaines, timber-framed sixteenth-century, and then across the little stream New Gaines and farther on again Hamish Park, both of brick. These houses are examples respectively of late seventeenth- and early eighteenth-century construction, evidence of brick becoming the most popular building material for the better-class house. New Gaines has been added to over the years to make a big brick house, mainly of eighteenth- and early nineteenth-century build, but containing a very graceful early Gothic Revival room and a library in Chinese style reminiscent of the Brighton Pavilion.

There is still a considerable area of common land in this part of Herefordshire, Bringsty on both sides of the main road almost linking up with Badley Wood Common and in the other direction with Bromyard Downs which again extends both sides of the main Worcester-Bromyard road. Economically their main use is as grazing for sheep, but the bracken-covered slopes are pleasant places in which to wander. Surprisingly, on a levelled area close to the road is a football pitch where in summer, after due rolling, cricket is played, an unusual sight on a bracken-covered hill. South of the road, hidden from the sight of the motorist down a grassy track, is an inn The Live and Let Live. Even today there is something rather mysterious about these downs and for that matter something rather eerie on a misty night. One word of warning to the motorist: sheep do stray on to the main road and can be rather dangerous.

Almost surrounded by these bracken-covered hills is the National Trust estate of Lower Brockhampton. From the entrance a drive passes through a park of fine trees past the little Gothic Revival church of 1798 and then down a steep, twisty hill before passing through woodland until, a mile and a half from the main road, the view opens out to reveal a beautiful example of medieval timber-framing. The house which was built probably early in the fifteenth century is surrounded by a moat which seems to have been a status symbol of that period rather than a form of defence. Sited over the moat is a timber-framed gatehouse built almost 100 years later than the house itself.

Before going into the house it is worth noting the timber-framing; it is in square panels in the hall and the ground floor of the wing, but on the front of the latter facing the visitor it is of close-set, vertical framing indicating the main room, the great chamber of the master of the house. In later houses this distinctive use of close-set framing is sometimes found in the whole of the wing.

Inside the house the visitor finds himself back almost 600 years, for here is the original great, open hall with all its fine timber roof almost intact. The main, central truss is of a type known as a base-cruck, a rare form of building of which only nine examples have so far been found in Herefordshire and less than 90 in the whole country. Two great curved timbers start from the ground, but instead of continuing to meet at the apex as in a cruck building they support a cambered collar which carries the actual roof structure. In this way an extra few feet were gained on the width of the hall and the rising gentry of the period gave themselves something grander than their neighbours. The roof timbers are cusped trefoils and quatrefoils and there is evidence just west of the central truss of a louvre through which the smoke escaped from the open hearth.

The hall is entered through a spere truss in which two great posts go up to the purlins and between which is an arch going up to the collar.

To the west of the house is the roofless Norman chapel. Here as at Wolferlow and Tedstone Delamere the local tufa, looking rather like a pale lava, is used. It is interesting to have an opportunity to look closely at this soft porous stone used so often by the local church craftsmen of the early medieval period. For those with time the National Trust provides maps and details of a nature trail through the estate.

From Lower Brockhampton the traveller can take the road across Bromyard Downs to rejoin the Frome valley. Two roads converging on Bromyard follow this, the eastern from Stourport, the western from Tenbury Wells. On the former, south of the road to Wolferlow a lane leads west to the churches of Tedstone Wafre. The older, ruined building again makes considerable use of tufa while the newer, Victorian church leaves the impression of having been built of children's building bricks.

Saltmarshe Castle, built in the Victorian era was pulled down in 1955, but the castellated east and west lodges still remain to give some idea of the appearance of the main building. The latter lodge is on a by-road to Edvin Loach where there is another ruined church with great blocks of tufa in the south doorway and window and even more interesting late eleventh-century herring-bone masonry. The view from the churchyard is very worthwhile especially towards the Malverns.

The same by-road continues north and west to join the Bromyard-Tenbury road just south of Collington. At one time there were two churches here, but in 1352 a number of petitioners from both parishes requested that they be joined because 'so great and grievous hath been the late pestilence and plague, and so diminished the number of men . . . that the revenues of both churches are scarce able to sustain one priest'. The church of Collington Minor became the new parish church because it was the better constructed, but parts of Collington Magna were still standing in the eighteenth century and finally in 1856 a new church was built in the centre of the parish, the one which had been in use for 500 years being on the eastern side.

Like all these Frome valley settlements Edvin Ralph is just a house or two by the church and here as at Martin's Castle at Collington is a deserted medieval homestead moat. The church and moat are approached along a lane from the main road and under the tower is one of the most important collections of monuments in the county. They are of early fourteenth-century date and some, probably all, commemorate the Edefen (Edvin) family. Finally there is an incised slab to Maud Edefen of a slightly later date; it is a rare example of a pardon monument, the bishop of Worcester promising 30 days pardon and the bishop of Hereford 60 to those saying a pater and an ave for the soul of 'Matil de Eddefen'.

There is local tradition that Maud was the Victim of a quarrel between a lord of Edvin Ralph and a lord of Edvin Loach. She is supposed to have rushed between them as they were duelling and was killed as a result. Both men are said to have fought on until each was mortally wounded. It is an old tradition for in 1656 it was written 'one of the lords of these two lordships had a faire wife for such they fought and killed one the other', but, whilst there is perhaps a substratum of truth in the story, it does not seem likely that these are the monuments of the people concerned.

The Frome skirts the eastern edge of Bromyard, the town lying on the hill above the river somewhat aloof from it. The valley, which north of the town is steep-sided and narrow, begins to widen out and a minor road runs quite close to the river from just east of the bridge at Bromyard. An even better way of approaching it is to turn south just beyond the tile works and hospital about a mile east of the town. This takes one along a gated road through fields and orchards and then suddenly down into the valley. Although there is very little actual woodland there is an overwhelming impression of trees whether it is in summer when they are in leaf or in spring when there is blossom seemingly everywhere.

Down here by the river is another ruined church, that of Avenbury. It is a twelfth-century building, again using tufa, and although restored in 1881 and still in good repair about 1930, it is now roofless and in ruins.

The road following the river twists and turns, climbs and dips, so that at times one is looking down on the Frome, at others right alongside it. Other little streams begin to join the river and other roads run up their valleys, or, more often, follow the spurs between them. One such road is that to Stanford Bishop and immediately opposite the junction is the Rumney Building. At first sight it looks like a field barn and indeed that is its use today, but a closer look reveals cut stonework and in any case most barns in this area are of timber-framed construction. This isolated building on this quiet hillside overlooking the valley was a school built in 1731 to serve the neighbouring parishes. It was largely rebuilt in 1826.

Stanford Bishop Church is set on a knoll overlooking its parish. Below it in the valley is an old road, probably Roman, and its crossing of the river gave the parish the first part of its name. Perhaps it was along this road that St Augustine came if the story of the chair in this church is true. In the chancel is a very early, simple chair of posts with boards slotted into them. It is probably medieval, but is said to be the chair used by St Augustine in 603 when he met the Celtic bishops at a point somewhere on the Marches. It was rescued in the 1880s after being thrown out to be burnt and was for a long time in the museum at Canterbury Cathedral. The wooden hinges are of a type used by Roman carpenters, but it is doubtful if the chair is more than about half its claimed age. The Court is quite a fine early eighteenth-century farmhouse, but in the farm buildings, now part of a hop-kiln complex, is the old solar with its fine, timbered, fourteenth-century roof.

After returning through orchards and hop-yards to the Rumney Building the road down the Frome valley can be followed until another junction leads off to Acton Beauchamp Church situated on its own at the western end of the parish. As a building it is unusual, for it is a late Georgian church, built in 1819, but in the south doorway of the tower is a most unusual re-used Saxon cross-shaft, probably dating from the 9th century, carved with scroll work, a bird and animals.

The next section of the valley is known as the Golden Valley, not to be confused with the subject of a later chapter. Here for the first time is a really recognizable village at Bishop's Frome with a school, church and massive range of hop-kilns all close to the village green, round which the main road curves in two very sharp bends. Architecturally the church will not detain anybody very long, but the fifteenth-century rood-screen, the seventeenth-century chairs and the effigy of a late thirteenth-century knight in a recess in the south wall decorated with ball-flower ornament are all worth careful inspection. There are also three Italian paintings found behind the altar in 1974 after having been lost for a number of years. Two of them are attributed to da Messina (1444-93) and another, of the Virgin and Child with St John the Baptist, to Bonfiglio (1420-1500). These Italian paintings are completely unexpected in an English medieval church.

Here one is in the heart of the Frome valley for Bishop's, Halmond's, Castle and Canon Frome are clustered together and of these the first might be said to be the main village in the valley. It is bigger than the others and more obvious. Castle Frome would be missed completely were it not for the fact that the nineteenth-century, timber-framed bell-turret shows up from the main road against the trees on the hill behind. The castle is another quarter of a mile up the hill, now hidden by trees. In the church is a piece of sculpture which would draw attention anywhere in Europe. It is the font, one of the latest of the works of the Herefordshire School of carving. It probably dates from the third quarter of the twelfth century. Appropriately, the main subject on the bowl, which forms one piece with the stem, is the baptism of Christ. St John, the hand of God, and the Holy Dove are there with Christ in a tiny pool with fish in it. The symbols of the four evangelists and two doves complete the main band of carving between plaited ornament on the top and loose interlace below. The whole is supported by three, massive, crouching figures, two badly damaged, but one of them apparently a lion. It is a tremendously moving piece of sculpture. The fine Unett altar tomb of the early seventeenth century and the later slate wall tablet to the same family show that the carvers' arts did not die in the intervening 500 years.

Canon Frome is a big, late eighteenth-century brick house built by the Hoptons. The small Victorian church with a brick tower of *c.* 1680 is an important building designed by Bodley in 1860 while he was still very young. The glass in the rose window is of a remarkably high quality for that period. The Hopton family moved here from Shropshire at the turn of the sixteenth century. The house was garrisoned for the Royalists during the Civil War, but was taken on 22 July 1645 by Leven and his Scots when Colonel Barroll and 70 of his garrison were put to the sword. It was then garrisoned by the Parliamentarians, the first governor being Edward Harley. The Hopton family repossessed it after the war and was here until the county purchased the house to use as a school.

On the hill overlooking the river and Canon Frome is Ashperton. On the west side of the main road, by the church, are traces of the castle of the Grandison family. Their niche in history was assured when Katherine lost her garter and it was returned to her by Edward III with the famous remark, 'Honi soit qui mal y pense'. As a result the Order of the Garter was founded. The family also made its mark in history through Katherine's brother, John, who became bishop of Exeter and was responsible for the magnificent Decorated architecture of the great cathedral there. On the west side of the village street is an easily seen example of a cruck house.

In the valley to the east of the village is a well-preserved stretch of the Hereford-Gloucester Canal which was completed in 1845. One end of a tunnel can be seen on the north side of the road to Bosbury and towards Stretton Grandison the embankment is still clearly visible across the fields.

The latter village is situated on the opposite side of the Frome valley from Ashperton on a series of bends on the hill. Towards the western end of the village is a fine barn on the south side of the road

7. Henry Holland's beautiful drawing room and ceiling at Berrington Hall

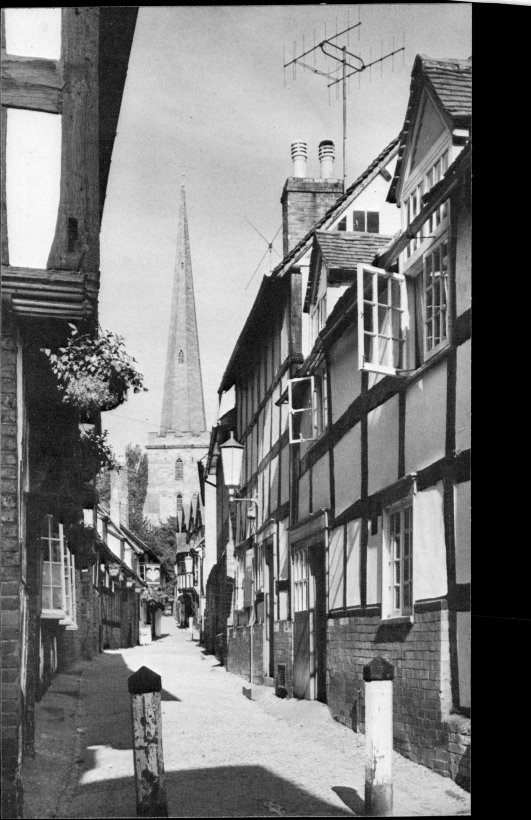

with its heavy wattling still complete. This type of walling, never intended to be plastered, was ideal for barns for it allowed ample ventilation, but still made a more or less solid wall. The farmhouse, west of the barn, is a good example of brick coming into use as the main material for the better-class house in this county *c.* 1700. The minor road to the east past the church is worth following for the delightful run along an unfenced road through parkland with fine trees. The church itself contains armour and monuments of the Hoptons, and the murals of a lady over the south doorway and a badly mutilated St Christopher opposite are unusual in this county.

Here one is in the valley of the Lodon, a tributary of the Frome on the banks of which are the Cowarnes, Much and Little, and Stoke Lacy. In Much Cowarne Church is a late thirteenth-century mutilated effigy of a knight said locally to be Grimbald Pauncefoot of Pauncefoot Court. Silas Taylor writing during the Commonwealth period describes an effigy of a woman alongside this with 'her left arm couped above the wrist in memory and confirmation of her heroic conduct'. This female figure has long since disappeared, but 'her heroic conduct' is supposed to be that as ransom for her husband who had been taken prisoner on a crusade Constance had her left hand cut off and sent it in payment for his release. A similar story is told about Pauncefoot tombs at Crickhowell in Breconshire and Hasfield in Gloucestershire. How far the story is true it is difficult to tell today and here in this quiet, peaceful church such happenings seem far away. Part of the moat at Pauncefoot Court immediately east of the church still exists, but the house of Grimbald and Constance has disappeared.

Below the confluence with the Lodon the valley of the Frome widens out again. North of the river are Yarkhill, Weston Beggard and Bartestree. At the first named lived Fabian Stedman the famous campanologist. Built into the church porch is a fourteenth-century churchyard cross with a Crucifixion with the Virgin and St John.

Like Yarkhill, Weston Beggard is off the main road right down by the river. These two parishes are completely missed unless a definite effort is made to get to them. In the church is a sumptuous

8. Church Lane, Ledbury

early fourteenth-century tomb recess in the south wall of the chancel with a crocketed gable and cusped and sub-cusped arch with spandrels carved with foliage and shields. Opposite is a much simpler recess of probably slightly later date decorated with ball-flower ornament.

The small parish of Bartestree is dominated visually by the Convent of Our Lady built in brick in 1863 in typically Pugin Gothic, and added to in 1881, 1889 and 1895. The convent chapel is the fourteenth-century chapel of Old Longworth house which was for a long time used as a barn, but was restored in 1860.

Across the river are Tarrington, Stoke Edith and Dormington. At the first named the church still preserves a section of its Norman apse which was excavated in 1931. In the chancel north wall is an early fourteenth-century effigy of a lady in a gown and cloak in a quite elaborate recess with ball-flower ornament, a gabled label with crockets and side pinnacles with finials. This is a more complete village with its Court, church and the late Georgian Foley Arms.

Stoke Edith is now virtually a place of the past. The church and the elegant eighteenth-century rectory are still there, but the great house was burned out in 1927 and later taken down. Celia Fiennes described the house as nearly completed in 1698 and it was a beautiful brick building of that period with stone dressings. Its destruction is a considerable loss to the architecture of Herefordshire. The Foley family and lovers of good design in building have been unfortunate in that the two great houses of these seventeenth- and eighteenth-century ironmasters, Stoke Edith and Great Whitley in Worcestershire were both burnt out. The church was rebuilt by the Foleys in 1740-42 and is one of the few examples in the county of that century. The Foley monuments and the three-decker pulpit are typical of the period, but there is also a late fifteenth-century alabaster effigy of a lady, probably a Walwyn. The lodges of Stoke Edith, especially the west lodge on the main road, are worth more than just a glance in passing. The western is octagonal of brick with a copper dome and Tuscan columns to impress the approaching visitor. The Foleys did not hide their wealth and importance.

These last three villages in the valley are also on the northern edge of the Woolhope Hills and geologists will want to visit the disused quarry at Perton to see some of the exposures of the Silurian rocks. This is great fossil-hunting country beloved of geologists and schoolboys, a pastime now very much discouraged in the interests of conservation.

Dormington makes a pleasant group of court, church and rectory, the first partly timber-framed, partly brick. Set back from the road is the hamlet of Prior's Frome, the last of the places to take its name from the river and above it is Back Bury Hill. One should climb up to this fort where Ethelbert is supposed to have camped before moving on to Sutton Walls and his murder. The view over the meandering of the Wye and the Lugg through the rich farm lands, past the towers and spires of Hereford to the dark, distant hills is worth the climb. From here looking down over the confluence of the Frome and Lugg and on to where the latter joins the Wye it is clear why the bridge at Mordiford became so important as a way into Hereford. In the other direction is a wonderful panorama of the geological faults and upheavals which make up the Woolhope Hills.

One aspect of the valley which can be seen from this viewpoint is the importance of hops to lowland Herefordshire and its scenery, not just in the sight of the long straight lines in the hop-yards, but in the contribution made by the hop-kilns rising from the farmyards. In some of the older houses there is still a hole in the floor of an upper room, sometimes just inside the front door, from which the hop-sack used to be hung. A man would climb down into this and tread down the hops as they were tipped in around him, emerging thirsty, dusty and hot at the top some hours later with seven feet of packed-down hops beneath him. Today this is a mechanical process. Hop-picking used to be a time when hundreds of people from the great conurbations descended on the county for a few weeks and they and their caravans made a striking picture. In some areas special hutted accommodation was built for them. However, the last two decades have seen the virtual end of the human hop-picker. Today the bines are picked mechanically, brought into the farmyard and stripped by machine before being dried in the modern temperature-controlled kilns. This process has always been the most important in the cycle. The kiln was close to the house, in the early examples almost always adjoining it, in order that the farmer might turn the hops at intervals and closely watch the drying. A few of these early wattle-and-daub kilns still exist, one or two of them dating from *c.* 1700. Hop growing seems to have started in the county in the first half of the seventeenth century, constant reference being made to it in the inventories of dead peoples' goods from that time onwards.

From here on Back Bury one overlooks the end of the Frome valley, the 'Frummy' as it is still sometimes known locally. In spite of the fact that the main Hereford-Worcester road follows the valley for some miles it is still little known for most of its length. The villages are small, there is no outstanding church architecturally, there are a number of ruined churches and very little use of the wealthy ball-flower ornament in their decoration, yet most of it is a wealthy valley. There are good quality farmhouses for all its length from Dudshill Court near the source to Prior's Frome overlooking the confluence. It is almost a contradiction; the magnificent carving of the font at Castle Frome, the cross at Tedstone Delamere and the nineteenth-century glass at Canon Frome are important in any county of architectural treasures, but they have to be looked for. This delightful valley still hides its treasures, not secretively, but in an unassuming way, taking them for granted as part of the surroundings. Its scenic beauty, its farms, its churches and its little villages are there to be enjoyed. They are mainly on a small scale and perhaps the word gems can be aptly applied to them.

THREE

Down the Wye from Hay to Hereford

Some years ago the writer was leading a group recording buildings in the Ewyas Lacy Hundred and found one of his students happily sketching some in Hay, oblivious of the fact that she had strayed over the border into Wales. Just as easily and without noticing it the traveller passes from Breconshire into Herefordshire. The suburbs of Hay are in England, officially part of the parish of Cusop, just as part of Presteigne, which is in Radnorshire, is across the Arrow in Stapleton.

Of all the entries into Herefordshire from Wales the route past Hay Castle and along the Wye to Hereford is probably the best loved by travellers. Two roads run beside the river, that on the northern bank being the more important, and both give beautiful views of the Wye and pass through lovely villages. There is a good, modern bridge at Hay, but it is probably better for the traveller who wants to explore this part of Herefordshire to stay on the east bank of the river and cross by the toll bridge at Whitney.

The stream in Cusop Dingle is the boundary between England and Wales and Cusop Church and Castle stand overlooking the bridge which carries the road which crosses into Wales, then divides to go one way to Llanthony the other back into England to Longtown. Very little is left of the castle, but the church has a remarkable scissors-braced nave roof. It is of heavy timbers, completely different from scissors-braced trussed-rafter roofs found in the east of the county. It is much more closely related to the roofs at Weobley and Bredwardine and at Porth Aml and Glasbury in Breconshire.

Whilst Cusop and its church and castle are hidden away in their wooded dingle a mile from the road, Clifford village and castle are obvious to all in the narrow gap between the road and the river. There was a borough and castle here at the time of Domesday and something of the street layout can still be traced from those early days. Of the castle, the keep, 150 feet above the river, still stands out in its ruined form, the hall with its undercroft, the twin towers of the gatehouse and three wall towers being clearly visible on the great motte. The whole site occupies about three and a half acres and in recent years a barbican has been excavated where the outer bailey must have been divided from the inner. The castle, which was destroyed in 1402 by Glyndwr, was immortalized by Tennyson in his *Dream of Fair Women* where he tells the story of Jane Clifford, 'Fair Rosamund', mistress of Henry II.

Between the castle and the river, on a terrace well below the keep, ran the railway from Hereford to Hay, Brecon and Builth Road, following the line of an earlier tramway for much of its route. The latter had been opened from Brecon to Hay in 1816 and continued to Eardisley in 1818 from where it was extended to Kington and the limestone quarries at Dolyhir. The tramway was bought up by the railway company in 1863. Later the Golden Valley railway was linked to this and the extensions to Builth Road gave access to the mid-Wales line. Today it seems strange to think of this network of routes; there is now no railway connecting Hereford with any place to the west, except via Abergavenny and Newport though the mid-Wales line from Craven Arms still exists.

The church at Clifford is on the hill half a mile from the castle at the old settlement of Llanvair. In it is one of the two wooden effigies to be found in the county, almost as far away from each other as they can be, for the other is at Much Marcle. Of a priest in mass vestments, it probably dates from the late thirteenth century and has been reputed to be of the founder of Clifford Priory. This seems unlikely as the priory was founded in the reign of Henry I and stood south of the church where Priory Farm is today, a little of the monastic building having been incorporated in the seventeenth-century house and one of the barns.

Up the hill from the church is Longhouse, now modernized, but partly timber-framed and at one time having been house and farm buildings under a long, continuous roof. Timber-framing is less common in this part of the county where stone is more readily available. From here a road runs out past the small, simple, Calvanistic Methodist Chapel towards Castleton Barn and it is along here that a malthouse has been converted into a dwelling. The tall building looks odd until one realizes its origins. Below is another road which winds its way out to a landing-place on the river. It is not the sort of road for those in a hurry, but for the traveller with a little time it is well worthwhile for the views over the Wye to the hills to the north and west. The castle from which Castleton takes its name is now a ruined motte down by the river.

Only just over a mile away is the third castle in Clifford parish guarding the entrance to this area. It is Newton Tump, a motte and bailey, on the line of a minor road from the Wye valley to that of the Dore standing almost on the watershed between the two.

The main road from Hay through Clifford reaches the Wye at the toll bridge just downstream from the now destroyed railway viaduct. It stands on wooden posts dating from *c.* 1820, a rather rickety-looking structure, which nevertheless seems to cope perfectly adequately with modern traffic. The tariff on the board outside the little toll-house on the north bank is in itself a piece of economic and social history.

The road to the left follows the river for two miles to the boundary with Wales, where, just in England, almost like a Customs House, stands the Rhydspence Inn. It is an attractive timber-framed building of sixteenth-century build and, unusually for this area, the timbers are close-set. With its jettied porch and some of its original windows still *in situ* it is a building for the expert as well as the photographer. At one time there was a ferry across the river below the inn, but it was important also as being on the route of the cattle drovers taking their animals from Wales to London 'on the hoof'. More recently it has been a rendezvous on Sundays for thirsty Welshmen unable to get a drink on their own side of the border.

The parish of Brilley rises from just over 200 feet above sea level down by the river to over 1,000 feet on Milton Hill, through woodland and farmland to rough grazing at the top. There is a wonderful collection of houses, both stone and timber-framed, some of them very early, many of them of west of England cruck construction.

One farmhouse, the Cwmma, is the property of the National Trust and is open on certain days. It is to be recommended to anybody who wants to see what a Herefordshire timber-framed farmhouse is really like. It is a box-framed house, a rectangular timber box with heavy, triangular roof trusses placed on it. The walls are of typical, Herefordshire, square-panelled timber-framing, there are star-shaped early seventeenth-century chimneys, a local stone roof and, very much a hill feature, a pentice roof projecting for about two feet at first-floor level. The rooms are well looked after and furnished and it is possible to examine in some detail the panelling, the stone fireplaces, the carpenters' assembly marks at the joints and in the roof the great principal rafters and purlins. The plan of hall, screens, service was beginning to break down when this house was built in the seventeenth century, but is still just being observed. Adjoining to the east is an earlier house, now doing duty as a cowhouse, with painted ceilings reminiscent of Scotland. The view from here and even more from the hill above is magnificent, from the Brecon Beacons to the Black Mountains to the Malverns and down the Wye valley. At the top of the drive is the Welsh boundary and the Roman road to Little Mountain Camp.

Brilley Church stands 400 feet above the river with a fine view from the churchyard in which there is a tombstone to a barge owner, an interesting confirmation of the river trade on the Wye. The church is the only one in the county with a baldacchino over the altar to protect it. It is similar to that in the neighbouring Welsh parish of Michaelchurch on Arrow and a very unusual feature in an English church.

A steep descent takes the traveller back to Whitney, the first of a series of villages built on the edge of the flood plain of the Wye. How close to the edge is perhaps summed up in the fact that most of the parish church was washed away in 1720 with the result that there is quite a Georgian flavour about the rebuilt edifice of 1740. Except for the Boat Inn, more evidence of river trade, the modern village is back from the river on a side road overlooked from the hill by the great, neo-Tudor pile of Whitney Court, built between 1898 and 1902. Here also is a tram wharf. Today we should call it a siding, but the old term was borrowed direct from the river trade which it usurped.

The next village along the river is Winforton, again with a tram wharf, but what catches the eye here is the timber-framing. As the traveller enters the village from the west on the south of the road is Winforton Court with diagonal bracing forming lozenges and two fine barns. Among the other black-and-white houses the one that stands out is Cross House with a pair of great, curved timbers forming a cruck-truss in the gable facing the road. The top stage of the church tower is timber-framed; this predominance of black-and-white is in contrast with Brilley just up the hill and Clifford across the river.

Willersley is a church and a house, or rather two houses, for the former has been declared redundant and converted into a dwelling. The other houses in the parish are much closer to Eardisley. The apparently eighteenth-century brick Willersley Court, the only house near the old church, is in fact a timber-framed hall and two cross-wing house built 200 years earlier.

Farther back from the river is Eardisley, a bigger, more important village, with its church and castle standing together at the south end of the village street. The former is bigger than most Herefordshire churches and the architectural development from the late twelfth century is worth following. However, there must have been a church here before this for the font is a magnificent example of the

Herefordshire School of carving and probably dates from *c.* 1150. It is almost certainly the work of the same craftsman as carved that at Castle Frome. There is interlacing on the top of the bowl and a knot pattern on the stem, while the main band of carving shows the harrowing of hell, two men fighting, one with a sword and the other with a spear, and a lion, a splendid animal with its tail flung up between its legs and over its head. The other unusual feature was a sallet of late fifteenth-century date which still has some remains of its leather lining and brass rivets. It is said to have been found at the castle and until recently hung on the east wall of the nave with another, later, helm.

The castle mound is just west of the church. The *domus defensabilis* mentioned in the *Domesday Book* presumably stood here. Today the bailey site is occupied by an early eighteenth-century brick farmhouse with a shell hood over the doorway. To the north of the church is an excellent example of good conservation where a nine-bay timber-framed barn has been converted into a pleasant row of cottages.

Opposite the church is the brick, Victorian school and from here for over a quarter of a mile runs the main street of the village. It is worth walking along this just to enjoy the variety of the buildings and the village atmosphere. There is Victorian and Edwardian brick, there is timber-framing from the fourteenth century onwards, there is weather-boarding and corrugated iron. On its way it crosses two streams, one of them with a jettied house hanging over it. On the east side one house with diagonally set stacks is bound to catch the eye and on the other The Forge is probably over two centuries older and inside has cruck trusses with the very early passing wind-braces. At the end of the street is the Tram Inn, for Eardisley was the terminus for a time of the tramway from Hay and later the Kington tramway ran from here through that town to the stone quarries beyond. Around the corner just beyond the chapel and the pump is a tiny, two-bay, cruck cottage with its crucks in the east gable for all to see.

The showpiece is Upper House Farm on the main road to

Kington just beyond the end of the village street. The original open hall is hidden from the road by an added seventeenth-century block, but enough can be seen from the road in passing to make this a fitting end to a memorable village.

The parish of Eardisley extends in all directions with little hamlets or townships each with its own special character. On Hurstway Common is the 'Great Oak' about 30 feet in girth and over 100 feet in height. At the Quebb are two cruck farmhouses opposite a still earlier site, now simply a series of bumps in the ground, Apostles has two cruck houses in the same farmyard and Lower Welson is a very attractive township. At Bollingham, over two miles north of the village, is the medieval chapel which served this northern part of the parish.

From Eardisley a road runs to Almeley and for much of the way the track of the old tramway runs alongside it as a bank by the side of the road. It is in a good state of preservation and shows very well how these early nineteenth-century tramways looked.

In Almeley village the church, castle mound and manor house make a fine group. The church is a fine clerestoried building rebuilt in the years about and just after 1300, but still retaining the tower of the church built about a hundred years earlier. The painted ceiling of the eastern two bays of the nave over the rood-screen with a Tudor rose in the centre of each panel is an unusual feature in Herefordshire churches and dates from the early sixteenth century.

The motte and bailey of the castle stands to the south-west of the churchyard, while to the north is the manor house, a striking late medieval building looking down over its formal garden across the road to the churchyard. The parlour end, nearest the village, has close-set framing, often used in this area to mark the most important room or rooms, and the porch is jettied. The panels are infilled with brick which may be a replacement of earlier wattle and daub.

The road north from the village leads to the township of Almeley Wooton where there is a timber-framed Friends' Meeting House built in 1672 and given to the Society three years later. Its peace and simplicity in its well-kept enclosure make an impression which seems to belong to this quiet, delightful countryside with its small villages and scattered townships. The Quakers had a number of Meeting Houses in the county, Ross, Leominster, Hereford and Almeley being the main centres. The important families in the movement were the Prichards, originally of Almeley; the Southalls and Newmans of Leominster, the Cowles and the Merricks of Ross who had Quaker connections all over England and Wales and in America. Edward Prichard of Almeley spent some time in Pennsylvania and then returned to Almeley in the early eighteenth century. A number of families in the USA today trace their ancestry back to the Friends from Herefordshire.

From Almeley a road leads to Kinnersley with its castle and church. Castle is a misleading word to describe the fine late Elizabethan and early seventeenth-century house to be seen in the park immediately east of the church today. It is rather a medieval fortified manor, a tower house really, much altered and added to at that time with still later additions. Very rare for the west of the British Isles are the brick, crow-stepped gables more usually associated with the eastern side of the country and the Low Countries. Most of this modernization and addition seems to have been the work of Roger Vaughan who bought the estate *c.* 1588. It is now a Home for the Elderly and in it there is still some very fine late sixteenth-century plasterwork, particularly in the upper drawing room. There is here the common tale of a secret passage, but as it is supposed to run to the church only a few yards away this is more likely to be true than most such stories, though in fact, it is probably a drainage system.

From outside the most prominent feature of the church is the massive north-west tower built probably about the middle of the fourteenth century. Its sheer, unbuttressed outline and saddle-back roof give it a rugged, but impressive appearance. Inside, the monument erected in 1635 by the then owner of the castle, William Smalman, to his parents is perhaps the most noticeable piece of work, but beneath it and dwarfed by it is a good brass to William Leviot, rector of Kinnersley, who died in 1421.

Again this is a parish of small townships. From the church it is worthwhile going west, passing a good example of cruck construction on the north side of the road, and then turning south to Ailey and on to Letton. In the old Mason's Arms at Lower Ailey there is the unusual feature of a series of prayers painted on the walls. Close to the old railway station there were until recently some strips in an open field still held as in medieval times. Consolidation was being talked about and it seems as though another hardly-known relic of the agricultural past is about to disappear.

From Ailey down to the river, two miles away, is an area which has been liable to flooding for hundreds of years. It is known as Letton Lakes and in spite of modern drainage there are still times when it is under water. By the main road at Letton is Bull Farm, a recent, post-office Georgian house on a mound overlooking the site of the old farm which was demolished a few years ago and which had on its walls a series of plates marking the flood level at various times from 1715 to 1963. It is a wonder it was lived in so long. Half a mile along the road is Bridge Farm, where the cooking range is on a platform about three feet above floor level. It is not surprising that it has not been lived in for some years.

The church at Letton has some early Norman walling and, again, tufa is used. However, the most interesting work of that period is the carved lintel of the south doorway. It is mainly a geometric pattern, but on the east side are four roundels, two with heads with rays around them and two of creatures which appear to represent Cancer and Scorpio. All four figures, the first two being probably the moon and the sun, appear to have been copied from a medieval manuscript containing calendar illustrations. The door itself is a very early one dating from *c.* 1200, nail-studded, with strap hinges with curved arms and scrolls. Together the doorway and door form an outstanding example of work of the period. In the church the pulpit is a splendid early eighteenth-century example and the rich ball-flower ornament of four centuries previously occurs on a recess in the transept.

Brobury, on a minor road from Letton, overlooks a long bend in the river. It is virtually a deserted village. The church has been declared redundant and is being converted into a house and the late timber-framed cottages on the road to the Scar are deserted and decayed. The path through the wood at this latter spot opens out on to a fine view down the Wye. For those with time a walk along the same bridle-path leads to the avenue of magnificent trees at Monnington.

From the Scar the road leads back to the main Portway on the line of the Roman road at Staunton-on-Wye. However, it is better to cross this and follow the minor road to the village, a pleasant mixture of timber-framing, stone and brick, of thatch, stone tiles and slate. For those with time it is worth following the aptly-named Duck Street and the path beyond it to World's End. Alternatively one can go down to Little London and follow a path to Pig Street in Norton Canon parish. These strangely named little settlements are the results of enclosure at various times from the seventeenth century onwards. Gradually they have enclosed the common moorland which is the eastward extension of Letton Lakes. In days before modern drainage and farming methods, eking a living out of this easily flooded land must have been a precarious business. Some of the houses are wonderful examples of how to start with one or two rooms and add and add in whatever materials became available.

In the village is an unusual example of a complete social services establishment founded in 1790 under the will of George Jarvis to help the parishes of Staunton, Bredwardine and Letton. As the result of an Act of Parliament in 1852 for administering the charity a school was built and also almshouses for six men and six women, a house for the medical officer and a house for the clerk or quartermaster. After the founding of the National Health Service the doctor's house was no longer needed and part of the school building is now a Youth Hostel.

Along the street towards the eastern end of the village is the seventeenth-century Lower House Farm on the north side of the road with its 1963 replacement on the south. Unusually, a little farther along is its predecessor of *c.* 1500, built originally as a hall or living room with direct access to a byre alongside. Later the hall was divided by a floor and additions made to the house, but the byre with direct access from the living room continued in use into this century. It has now been restored, but in the process has lost its original stone roof which was getting 'tired', i.e. was beginning to let in the rain. The church at the east end of the village is basically Norman.

Norton Canon about two miles to the north is worth a visit to see the brick church of 1716, a most unusual structure for this county, erected at a time of very little church building. A surprising feature is the careful re-use of the thirteenth-century windows.

Strangely the church at Monnington-on-Wye on the opposite side of the Portway, is also a complete late building, having been rebuilt in 1679 by Uvedale Tomkins of Monnington Court. Only the tower survives from the Perpendicular church. It is a fascinating example of a church of the reign of Charles II whose arms are on the wall, with twisted balusters in screen and altar rails typical of the period, still lit by oil lamps. Just outside the porch is a broken slab reputed to mark the burial place of Owen Glyndwr, the last crowned Prince of Wales, whose daughter, Margaret, was the wife of Roger Monnington.

The Court, alongside, looks like a seventeenth-century stone house, and indeed most of it is, but the wing nearest the church is either a fifteenth-century first-floor hall, or, more probably, the great chamber in the cross-wing of an earlier house. Its fine original roof still survives. It is from here that a magnificent avenue of Scotch Firs runs north-west looking towards the Scar near Brobury; it was probably planted in 1628 to mark the election of William Tomkins as MP for Weobley. The drive along this leads to an old crossing of the river, originally by ferry, but from 1868 to 1962 by a gothic cast-iron bridge which had to be taken down after flood damage.

Here one is in the heart of the Wye valley, very good farmland: grain growing, Hereford cattle and, on the hills, timber. The wealth of this area is shown in the number of fine farm and manor houses on both sides of the river from here right down to Chepstow.

Back on the Portway a link road leads north to the Hereford-Kington road passing beneath Garnons Hill and through Mansell Gamage. Here in the trees is another redundant church, the third already in this valley. In the hamlet, for it is not really a village, are timber-framed houses including a manor house of the early seventeenth century and also some estate houses built probably late in the last century with applied timber to keep the black-and-white appearance.

Garnons house and park overlook the main road beautifully set between the hill and the farmland leading down to the river. The wood contains some magnificent oak trees, one grove having a number rising to 120 feet. There are also fine trees in the park, landscaped by Repton in 1791, and Sir Richard Cotterell carries on the interest in trees and forestry about which more will be written under Queen's Wood. The siting is superb and the house, built in 1860 on to an earlier part of 1815 and replacing an Elizabethan mansion, fits well into it. Repton would surely be delighted if he could see the picture today.

Opposite the park is the road down to Byford Common, a typical collection of late, timber-framed, squatters' houses. Farther along is the Victorian brick school and the cricket field with its timber-framed pavilion, typical of good nineteenth-century estates.

Between the main road and the river is Byford, an earlier crossing place of the Wye. The church, opposite the Court, is partly Norman while the tower is as late as 1717, but perhaps the best work in it is in the 'stiff leafed' capitals of the south transept. The Court is another of these fine manor houses to be found along this valley. Originally timber-framed it is now almost completely cased in stone and over the wall can be seen the top of the dovecote.

Just east of Byford the main road crosses Offa's Dyke which for a short distance here is quite massive, though for most of lowland Herefordshire it is virtually non-existent.

A little farther east is Bridge Sollers, where there is still a crossing of the Wye. The little Norman church overlooking the bridge has a twelfth-century doorway with imposts carved with a dragon on one

9.   Ross-on-Wye from across the river

side and two monsters and a head on the other, another example of the Herefordshire School of carving. The view from here across the river to Hay Bluff and the Black Mountains is superb.

From the crossroads a road leads north to the old Roman road running west from Kenchester. The main village of Bishopstone lies along this, but the old settlement of church and court lie farther north. The church was considerably restored in the late seventeenth-century and has an intricate king-post roof of that date. To the specialist the organ built in 1700-1701 and brought here in 1844 from Eton College is of considerable interest.

Bishopstone Court, north of the church, still has its ruined gateway, built c. 1600, and a good, deep moat with plenty of water in it. When the rectory was being built in 1812 close to the present village, a Roman mosaic pavement was found and considerable remains of that period.

North of Bishopstone the main Hereford-Kington road is reached and it is worth going along this to the west for a short distance to Yazor and then turning north through the woods to Yarsop. Here one is at the head of the Yazor Brook in a quiet, peaceful valley surrounded completely by wooded hills. It is a delightful spot, away from the modern world. The brook runs through Mansell Lacy, Kenchester, Stretton Sugwas and Huntington to Hereford where it joins the Wye. Here also close to Yarsop, above the Yazor, stood Foxley, a fine, square, brick house built in 1717 and unfortunately demolished. Sir Uvedale Price, perhaps the most brilliant of the protagonists of the English Picturesque, lived here and much of his planting remains. Even such distant prominent objects as the Skirrid and the Sugar Loaf near Abergavenny became focal points in his landscaping. Here in these peaceful surroundings during the war of 1939-45 was the 123rd American General Hospital and later a Polish resettlement camp.

The other end of the drive from Foxley led to the village of Mansell Lacy, but the traveller approaches it from the main road turning north by the now disused Victorian school. It is a lovely Herefordshire village, a number of timber-framed houses of varying

10. John Abel's town hall at Leominster, 1633

ages, an eighteenth-century brick manor house, a good church and
a stone and timber-framed post office. It is a village in which one
does not hurry. The church has grown and changed gradually with
work in it from each of the great periods of gothic building, a fine
east window of the early fourteenth century decorated inside and out
with ball-flower ornament and a good set of trussed-rafter roofs. On
the corner, north of the church, the post office has a full set of
doveholes in the gable of the stone cross-wing. Farther up towards
Merryhill Wood is the ruined chapel from above which is another
good view point back over the valley.

As the traveller approaches Brinsop Church he may well wonder
if he is trespassing, for it lies off a very minor road, across a green,
beautifully situated looking down over a tributary of the Yazor. It
is worth the adventure, for this church is one of the more interesting
in the county. Here the Norman carvers of the Herefordshire School
have given us on a tympanum St George on horseback with his
spear piercing the dragon, while on the voussoirs are fishes, birds,
animals and human figures and angels in the same cloaks with
pleated, parallel folds as in the other examples. However, there is not
only the carving, for St George appears in medieval stained glass in
the east window and there is twentieth-century glass by Comper as
well as a fourteenth-century rood-screen and the memorials in brass
and stone to the Daunsey family who lived at the Court.

The latter is one of the most remarkable buildings in
Herefordshire, a moated, stone, fourteenth-century manor house still
well preserved. In the south wing is the first-floor hall with its
magnificent crown-post roof. This is a most unusual form of construction in this county yet it is heavily cusped in the local style. One
wonders what is the story behind it; was it carved by a local man
who had spent some time in eastern England, or by a craftsman
brought in from further east, but who assimilated the local idiom?
It was at Brinsop Court that Wordsworth frequently stayed and
wrote sonnets descriptive of local scenes and events.

A mile away on a spur of Nupton Hill, built of the fine red
sandstone of the ridge on which it stands, is Hawk's Nest, a house

which looks as though it belongs to Devon or Cornwall, both from the colour of the stone and from the long mullioned windows in the gable. Those who long ago first named it because of its position could not have guessed that in the eighth decade of the twentieth century its owner and his hairdresser wife would keep three goshawks and a falcon which they have trained and which they fly over this beautiful stretch of country.

In 1887 some Roman pottery was found in a well at Brinsop, but the major Roman site of Herefordshire is at Kenchester down the valley. Here was the walled town of *Magnis,* suggesting in its shape ribbon development along the road from Gloucester to Clyro and Brecon. The north–south road to what seems to have been a bridge actually passes outside the defences. Houses and what may prove to be a temple have survived, with good tessellated pavements and hypocaust heating, though on the ground all that can be traced are the grass-covered walls and a few smaller mounds.

Probably Leland was right when he wrote, 'Of the decay of Kenchester, Hereford rose and florishyd'. What is not so sure is whether *Magnis* was the successor to the great hill-fort of Credenhill on the hill overlooking the villages. It was occupied from *c.* 390 B.C. until *c.* 75 A.D. and it seems probable that it was this town which moved to Kenchester and later to Hereford.

The village of Credenhill is now to a large extent lost in an RAF camp and the building consequent upon it, but the church with its fine porch and, surprisingly, a palm tree outside, is well worth visiting because of the stained glass in the north-west window. This dates from the fourteenth century and represents the two Sts Thomas, of Canterbury, and of Hereford. It must have been here that Thomas Traherne, one of the county's greatest poets and vicar of Credenhill from 1661-70 wrote, 'being seated among silent trees, and meads and hills . . . I chose rather to live upon ten pounds a year, and to go in leather clothes and feed upon bread and water, so that I might have all my time clearly to myself'. His poetry was lost for over two centuries, but now he ranks with Vaughan, Donne and Herbert as a great metaphysical poet. It is interesting to speculate what effect the Marcher countryside and their upbringing here had on these great poets.

The Roman road north-east from Credenhill leads under the great Iron Age fortress to Tillington, a township in the parish of Burghill. The main village is worth walking around on foot for it is a good mixture of timber-framed and later brick houses with good views away to the Black Mountains and Hay Bluff. West of the church was a moated site, which used to be claimed as the Anglo-Saxon 'burgh'. It has been ploughed out of existence, but seems to have been a medieval homestead rather than the original site of the village. The church has a handsome fifteenth-century rood-screen with a loft which projects six feet. This alone would demand a visit to the church, but so would the late twelfth-century font with its applied lead ornament and its carved stone base. To some the altar tomb with the alabaster effigies of Sir John Milbourne and Elizabeth *c.* 1440 would be the main attraction, but for others it would be the brass in the chancel with a globe, a coat-of-arms, the date 1619 and an inscription which reads, 'Here lyeth the bodye of Robert Masters, Gent. late Lord of this Mannour, who travelled with Thomas Candish Esqr to Virginia, and afertwards about the Globe of ye whole Worlde'. Thus in this village, so far from the sea is buried one of two Herefordshire men who accompanied Cavendish on his circumnavigation of the globe, the other being Robert Hughes of Little Hereford.

At Burghill one is getting close to Hereford and to the south on the line of the Roman road is Stretton Sugwas where once the bishops had a palace. Little is left of this now, a few stones and a Norman arch in the stable of Sugwas Court being the only evidence. The church also has been rebuilt, but its south doorway has been reset and has a superb tympanum of Samson and the Lion. It is another of the carvings of the Herefordshire School *c.* 1150 and seems to be by the same hand as Castle Frome font and St George and the dragon at Brinsop. There is in the nave a finely incised monument to Richard Grenewey and Maud (Harper), his wife, who died in 1473. It is a beautiful piece of work complete with an elaborate canopy and two dogs at the feet of Richard and Maud.

Between Stretton Sugwas and Hereford is the parish of Breinton. Like Hampton Bishop on the other side of Hereford, although so close to the city parts of it seem remote and completely rural. Only a few hundred yards from the city boundary is Warham Court, a farmhouse which still shows much of what it must have been like when first built in the fifteenth century. The cruck hall and original parlour wing still stand, but a fine close-set timber-framed addition was made to the latter *c.* 1600. Farther west is Warham House, a Queen Anne house completely encased and enlarged in Victorian times and Breinton Court where fine timber-framed barns show the importance and wealth of the farming in this part of the county. Early man left his mark in the defences, virtually a cliff-fort, between the church and the river.

It was on this low cliff and on the slightly higher land away from the river but with views over it, that late nineteenth and twentieth-century Hereford business and professional men built their villas, outside the city yet close enough to keep very much on top of their works and offices never more than about two miles away.

The western end of Breinton close to the Wye is different, for here is haphazard commons development of the late seventeenth century onwards, tiny houses, some timber-framed, some brick, which have 'just growed' and many of which are still along muddy lanes away from the surfaced road. This area is now changing rapidly as these houses of an earlier poor are bought and modernized by twentieth-century Herefordians.

It was at Breinton, a few years ago that the writer went to speak to the Women's Institute on Hallowe'en. There, down the lane at gateway after gateway were the mangolds with the pulp hollowed out and eyes, nose, ears and mouth cut out lit from the inside by a candle. It was fascinating to find this ancient custom still very much alive; it is one which in some parts of the country has been transferred a few days to Guy Fawkes night. It is yet another example of how our ancestors managed to keep the excuse for a night's fun whether it were pagan, or Christian or some other reason. Guy Fawkes could come under any of those headings depending on individual views.

From this strange mixture which is Breinton it is probably better to go back up river to Bridge Sollers to cross the Wye rather than go on to Hereford. This gives the traveller an opportunity to wander around the beautiful garden of The Weir with its views over the hills of Wales away to the south-west. This garden, belonging to the National Trust, is at its best in April and May, but is well worth a visit at any time.

Having crossed the river at Bridge Sollers the best plan is to turn left at Lulham and wander eastwards along the lanes close to the Wye to Eaton Bishop. On the way the Roman road from Aber-gavenny to Kenchester is crossed for those great builders crossed the river downstream from The Weir. Eaton Bishop was a small, untouched village until a few years ago, but it is now becoming a detached suburb of Hereford. It is still a very pleasant spot with the church, the brick Martin's Croft of *c.* 1700 and timber-framed barn forming an attractive group. The church of St Michael and All Angels is memorable for its stained glass which appears to have been the gift of Adam de Murimouth *c.* 1328 who is commemorated in the east window. This is the finest fourteenth-century glass in the county, perhaps a little more sombre with its brown, green and yellow than the more usual fifteenth-century glass with its blue and red. The archangel himself occupies one light, with his fellow Gabriel, in another, the Virgin and Child in a third and the Virgin and St John in the fourth. There is more stained glass of the same period in the north-east and south-east windows.

Down by the river is a tucking mill on the Case Brook and in the triangle at the confluence of the latter and the Wye is a fine promontory fort. There are good views up and down the Wye from here.

The lane leads on to Belmont, a fine eighteenth-century house almost entirely surrounded by nineteenth-century Gothic additions. This is the seat of the Wegg-Prosser family who also own the Victorianized Queen Anne house across the river in Breinton.

Perhaps the nineteenth-century work on Belmont House was never finished because of the amount of money the family spent on the great Benedictine church of St Michael built on their estate between 1854 and 1882. It was a cathedral from 1855 until 1920 and now is an abbey with an independent school attached. The Wegg-Prossers were well-known locally for their steam paddle-boat which they used on the Wye and which was brought to Hereford, minus its paddles, on a barge on the Gloucester-Hereford canal.

From the abbey the main road leads to Clehonger and Kingstone, both of which have grown in the last few years, much as Eaton Bishop has. 'Clunger', as it is called locally, lies just to the north of the main road, but is worth a detour for the fine series of effigies in the north chapel of the church. The most important of these is probably that of Sir Richard Pembrugge who founded the chantry in 1341. It is an altar tomb on which he lies in his armour, carrying his shield which bears his coat-of-arms, with his feet on a hound. On a smaller altar tomb lies a lady, probably his wife, with a large bird (a goose?) at her feet pulling on her cloak. In the same chapel are brasses to Sir John Barre who died in 1483 and his wife, Eden.

Kingstone has a centre, the church and the collection of houses around it, but because of hutted war-time camps it seems to lack a real core today. The church is architecturally not important, though the flowing tracery of the west window is unusual for Herefordshire, but the simple breccia font of the thirteenth century and the long 'dug-out' chest of about the same date are both interesting.

From Kingstone to Madley the land is very flat and we are in war-time aerodrome country. Soon there will be a big, dish aerial here for communications satellites. This countryside is big enough to take such changes and it will probably be no more a blot here than those at Goonhilly in Cornwall or, for that matter, Jodrell Bank in Cheshire.

Whichever way Madley is approached the great church dominates the scene. In the fourteenth century pilgrimages were made to a statue of the Virgin in the church and no doubt it was the offerings of the pilgrims which helped to build this beautiful and interesting place of worship. It is one of the country's bigger parish churches and it is surprising to find it here in this small, Herefordshire village. The nave and original aisles of thirteenth-century date show that a fine church and tower had replaced the earlier Norman building as early as this, but the fourteenth century added to this the chancel and crypt and then the north chapel. The chancel has that rare feature in England, a polygonal apse, and the falling ground at the east end made a crypt a natural development. The eaves cornice is decorated with the rich ball-flower ornament which appears again in the sedilia inside. The huge font is said to be the second biggest in England. In the east window are a series of stained glass roundels all apparently thirteenth century, a very early survival indeed. In the north, Chilstone, chapel, is a fine Renaissance tomb to Richard and Anne Willison, 1575. It is not unlike two tombs at Bosbury and bears the inscription 'This Towm John Gildo made'. The same John Gildon of Hereford was responsible for the Bosbury tombs. Every year this magnificent church is the scene of the Madley festival; once again the pilgrims flock to the village, not to pray at the statue of the Virgin, but to enjoy good music and help keep St Mary's in repair.

In the churchyard is one of the crosses of the type found in and near Herefordshire with a niche at the base, and one of the hazards of Madley is the cross at the road junction, which keeps getting damaged by cars whose drivers appear not to have seen it.

Tyberton, about three miles further west is a complete contrast to Madley. Here is a neat, brick church in an equally neat churchyard. The whole has the air of a wealthy estate and this is just what it was, for the church stands in what was once the grounds of Tyberton Court, a great house built by John Wood of Bath, in the years immediately after 1728, but now demolished. The church was built in 1719-21 and there does not seem to have been an architect as such. However, Wood was responsible in 1728-31 for the panelling behind the altar forming an internal apsidal east end. The festoons on this are symbols of the Passion and over the centre panel is the Holy Dove in Glory. This reredos is one of the most remarkable examples of English religious carving in the eighteenth century, yet strangely enough it has remained little known. The only work comparable to it is that in Redland Chapel in Bristol, but that was done some 15 years later and has not the same religious symbolism. At the south end of the churchyard is the timber-framed lodge to the now disappeared great house. This tidy, eighteenth-century scene is delightful at any time, but spring probably sees it at its best.

Blakemere is a series of twists in the main road; consequently the driver does not see it. It is worth parking the car and walking along a not too busy road and just lingering to look at the timber-framed houses and the church, rebuilt, but looking much the same as it must have done for hundreds of years, all set against the wooded backcloth of Blakemere Hill.

From here follow the minor road north-east to Ploughfield. In 1262 this was a borough. The hamlet today looks as though it has never been of importance, yet the big triangular green at the meeting of three roads must have been the market-place of the little town which never grew, just as at Richard's Castle and Dorstone. The modern village hall has perhaps taken the site of the old market cross or tolsey. Ploughfield is in the parish of Preston-on-Wye and in the little village around the parish church is another of the very rare base-cruck houses, built by some wealthy gentleman in the fourteenth century.

From Preston the lane continues, at times very close to the river, to Moccas. The Court, church, park and settlement of Moccas are between the road and the river, but the early castle mound and deer park are on the south-western side of the road. The church stands on its own on a mound in the park not far from the Court, but about a mile from the old castle. It is an almost perfect example of an early twelfth-century village church, completely Norman except for the enlargement of some of the windows. It is interesting to compare it with the much bigger and slightly later building at Peterchurch. There is the nave, a lower chancel and still lower apse. Apart from a little dressed sandstone the building is entirely constructed of tufa quarried locally. It is quite an experience to sit in this little church and realize that it is much the same now as it was 600 years ago. In this isolated bit of Herefordshire the peace, the atmosphere of the past can almost be felt. In all four fourteenth-century windows is contemporary stained glass in the form of splendid tabernacle work, each canopy containing two small figures. About the same age is the altar tomb in the chancel with its effigy of a knight in armour. The 1870 painting of the organ is unusual.

Moccas Court was built in 1775-81 by a local builder but to the designs of Robert Adam. It is a simple house with its climax internally in the circular room in a bow overlooking the Wye. The park was laid out by Capability Brown in 1778 and as late as 1803 Humphry Repton was working here. The time to see the great deer park beyond the main road is early evening when the deer come down from the woods to drink at the stream. Between the road and the park is a deer fence and leap so arranged that strange deer could leap into the park, but not get out. The fallow deer here are mainly menils, with the pale distinguishing mark on their rear ends. Some of the oak trees here are of 25 feet girth and more and to see the deer among these on a summer's evening is a real delight.

At Bredwardine is a crossroads where minor roads come down from Merbach Hill and up from the bridge over the Wye. On the west of the road looking down towards the bridge and the eastern wooded bank of the Wye is the Red Lion Inn, a very pleasant house of *c.* 1700 with a brick front, but rubble sides and back, and some of its windows still preserving their original wooden cross of single mullion and single transom.

The church and castle are down on the edge of the river, the nave of the former being one of the earliest pieces of surviving Norman work in the county with some herring-bone masonry in the north wall. Two recumbent effigies in the chancel are worthy of note. The one on the north side is of a knight in armour, probably a Baskerville, and dates from the fourteenth century, while the one opposite is a century later, of alabaster and probably of a Fouleshurst. The castle, south of the church, lies along the river cliff. Some excavation has been carried out in recent years, and has shown that it was of quite considerable importance. For those with time to walk a track follows the river from here to Moccas.

Probably the best-known incumbent of Bredwardine was Robert Francis Kilvert, the diarist, who was vicar here from November 1877, until his death in September 1879, and is buried in the churchyard. He was a native of Wiltshire and his first curacy when he came down from Oxford was in that county. From 1865 he was curate at Clyro for seven years and then, after another period in Wiltshire, he became vicar of St Harmon's in Radnorshire in 1876, moving to Bredwardine the following year.

The diary was kept from January 1870 until March 1879, and is a wonderful picture of rural life and society in the mid-Victorian period. It tells us much more about Wiltshire and Clyro than about Herefordshire, but shows an assiduous parish priest at work, a lover of the countryside who could describe the beautiful district in which he lived and the characters to whom he ministered. Sadly he died of peritonitis only a month after his marriage. He was a loss to his family and his parish, but he was a loss also to us, for if he had started again to keep his diary we should have had a very useful description of Herefordshire life in the late nineteenth century.

On the road down to Bredwardine bridge is Old Court which dates from the fourteenth century and still preserves its spere truss at the screens end of the hall and a scissors truss over the centre, a very rare type of roof similar to those at Glasbury and Porth Aml in Breconshire and to the remaining early truss in the church at Disserth in Radnorshire. It is a lovely stone farmhouse looking down over the river, where in complete contrast at the western end of the bridge is a small, late, timber-framed toll-house.

From here back to Whitney where the Wye was crossed at the beginning of this chapter is a beautiful stretch of the river. Go down onto the bridge and enjoy the views up river towards Letton with the cliff and woods on the east and the flat river meadows on the west, and down river towards Moccas past church and castle with the great ridge of Moccas Park and Woodbury Hill behind. Come back to the main road and follow it for some three miles to Clock Mills.

All the way the road is above flood level looking down over the river plain giving beautiful views first to the north and later to the west, with attractively situated farms at intervals by the roadside, again well above the levels the river sometimes reaches. At Clock Mills one is back in sight of Castleton and the journey is complete for those in a hurry, but for those who can spare the time the best view on this part of the Wye is yet to come.

At Bredwardine a road by the Red Lion leads up the hill. At the top where the road turns left a car can be parked and a track leads out through the bracken to Merbach Hill. Here at over 1,000 feet, on the edge of the bluff, is an almost aerial view along miles of the Wye valley. Away to the north are the hills of north Herefordshire and Shropshire and those of Wales to the west, below at the bottom is the flood plain, with no houses on it, but lots of lush grass, then the red arable soil and above that forest or rough pasture. Here one can see the wealth of Herefordshire, the grain-growing arable land, the meadows for fattening the cattle, and the forest. Also it is possible to realize the importance of this great natural gateway into and out of Wales and why through the ages the river and the roads on either side from Hay down to Hereford have carried armies and trade, cattle and visitors. This is surely the place to finish this journey along this great highway.

FOUR

The Arrow and Kington

Like the Lugg, into which it eventually flows, the Arrow rises in the hills of Radnorshire and takes its course down through Newchurch, past the trout farm at Michaelchurch between Little Mountain on the one side and Huntington on the other. On the former is a rectangular Roman fort with a road leading to it which still shows its original paving as one approaches the fortifications.

Huntington is the first Herefordshire village and its castle once guarded the route into Wales. The ruins still crown the motte by the roadside overlooking the market-place of the old borough. It is difficult today to imagine any sort of town here, but it could never have been very big. It has a peculiar kind of see-saw history with Kington which seems to have first achieved borough status in the twelfth century, while by *c.* 1230 there seems to have been an embryo borough at Huntington. However, in 1267 rents from 'New Kington' were nearly three times those from Kington. All three were clearly regarded for a time as having borough status.

There are the remains of two other castles in the parish. The church is tucked away behind a farmyard and should be visited if only to see the massive, rather primitive bench-ends. At Hengoed is an interesting school, closed in 1953. It was founded by Edward Goff, who was responsible for founding 12 other schools along the Marches. The Congregational Chapel and school stood here together.

This is an area still frequented by gypsies and a colourful reminder of these people is the collection of their caravans in the grounds of the Swan Inn at Huntington.

Off the road from Huntington to Kington a lane leads steeply down to Parkstile Mill which is still in working order. At Mahollam, behind the nineteenth-century farmhouse is a fine cruck house and behind that another school, disused since the early 1960s.

Down the hill from Mahollam are the remains of a wartime American hospital, an unexpected and incongruous sight in this lovely countryside.

Hergest Court is set upon a moraine in a commanding position looking over the flat bottom of the Arrow valley. Its most striking part externally is the close-set timbering of the northern wing, probably built in the seventeenth century, but the southern stone end of the house and the barn opposite are much earlier first-floor halls of the Vaughan family. They seem to be of fifteenth-century date. Earlier still is the motte and bailey on the opposite side of the road, Castle Twts. The house and family are famous because of the *Red Book of Hergest* found there by Lady Charlotte Guest and the black hound of the Vaughans. Many stories are told of this creature supposed to be the ghost of Black Vaughan and his appearance was said to herald a death in the family. There is more than one version of the story of the exorcizing of the ghost, but it seems that it was laid and imprisoned in a snuff box in Hergest Pool. There are certain similarities between this story and the Hound of the Baskervilles, made famous by Arthur Conan Doyle who is said to have been staying at Hergest Croft across the road from the Court when he wrote the story. A branch of the Baskervilles lived at Eardisley only a few miles away. On the opposite side of the road to Hergest Court is a series of watercourses controlled by a sluice-gate higher up the river. These could be used to irrigate the land and to flood it when necessary. The Vaughan family seem to have been pioneers in this technique and one of them was responsible for a very elaborate system in the Golden valley.

Margaret Vaughan of Hergest married Sir John Hawkins, the Elizabethan sea-dog, and left money to found a school at Kington.

The much-altered schoolhouse of 1625 is the first major building on entering Kington from Hergest. John Abel contracted to build it for £240.

Also on these western outskirts of the town is Hergest Croft, well-known for its flowering trees and shrubs and occasionally open to the public to raise funds for charities.

Kington is still a town in two parts. The old borough is up the hill away from the later development and has the church and castle mound, but the main town is on the low ground to the south. It is the only surviving Herefordshire market town which has never had representation in Parliament, its borough status apparently having been allowed to lapse very early in its history. However, it has been an enterprising town, having a tramway very early, planning a canal which never reached it and finally getting a railway, which it has lost in recent years.

The church, away from the modern town, is probably Norman in its origins, but its Early English chancel, built in the first few years of the thirteenth century, is perhaps its most attractive feature. It has a series of six small lancets on the north side, unusual in Herefordshire and reminiscent of Grosmont in Gwent. A curious and rare survival is the immersion pit alongside the Norman font. There is a similar and bigger example at Llanbister in Radnorshire, both presumably being relics of Baptist inclined clergy of the seventeenth century. Also in the church is the fine tomb chest with alabaster effigies of Thomas Vaughan and his wife, Ellen. He was killed at the Battle of Banbury in 1469. Both were well-known for their misdeeds, he being referred to as Black Vaughan and she as Ellen the Terrible. It is claimed that she avenged the murder of her brother by attending an archery tournament in disguise and then shooting an arrow at her brother's killer at point-blank range. The man she killed was a Vaughan; later she married his near relation.

To the north of the church a steep path descends past some medieval houses to the river. A few years ago during decoration some murals were discovered in one of these houses and the writer was asked to look at them. The plaster in every panel of a bedroom and landing had been painted, two motifs being used in the room in the quarterings of each panel. One was a simple, almost spherical vase of flowers, the other at first appeared to be a horse, but on closer examination the animal had antlers and presumably was intended to be a stag. On the landing a taller type of vase with flowers was the only motif. Black, blue and a little red were the colours used, the execution being so primitive that if ever there were do-it-yourself murals of *c.* 1600 these were they.

Below these houses is the mound of the castle commanding the valley of the Gilwern, a tributary of the Arrow. Down here, away from the town, is the route of the tramway and one of its bridges is still there carrying a footpath today. These horse-drawn tramways played an important part in the earlier years of the industrial revolution. Kington was linked to Hay via Lyonshall and Eardisley and from there a line went to Brecon. Later it was extended from Kington to Dolyhir. The line was complete by 1820. Coal was brought up from south Wales and grain, lime from Burlingjobb and Dolyhir quarries and some of the products of the local foundries were exported from the area by the tramway. The canal which had been planned to do this never got beyond Leominster. Later, in 1857, the railway replaced the trams and horses and was extended to New Radnor in 1876 but since the middle 1960s Kington has once again had to rely on road transport.

It is a town to linger in for a while and look at in detail. Down by the red brick market-hall, which in 1885 replaced John Abel's timber-framed building of 1654, notice the cast-iron curbstones, some are by Meredith of Kington others by Alexander and Duncan of Kington. Was this an attempt to share contracts fairly among local firms? As at Leominster there are two main hotels with assembly rooms, the Burton and the Oxford Arms. The former is red brick of 1851 and 1856 and even at that date simple Georgian. The latter appears to be Victorian, the front being heavily and elaborately stuccoed, but inside are the moulded beams of a seventeenth-century timber-framed building. As the Earls of Oxford, the great Harley

11. *above* Lower Brockhampton, moated early fifteenth-century house and later gatehouse; 12. *below* Clodoch Mill and Hatterall Hill

family, were staunch Whigs perhaps this assembly room was used by that party.

Along Duke Street, where the Oxford Arms is situated, are some good timber-framed houses and at the end where it becomes Victoria Road is the town's industrial area. Here by the river is the now disused railway station, the tramroad and the foundry built in 1820. At the time of writing a new light-industrial factory is being built in Kington.

As in so many country towns the Victorians showed their civic pride in public buildings. The market-hall has already been mentioed, but 40 years earlier a town hall had been built and whilst the premises is now shops the façade with its giant pilasters and pretty wreaths along the cornice still stands in High Street facing the visitor as he comes into the town up Bridge Street. This is so named because of the bridge at the other end where a big corn-mill is situated on the Arrow and a toll-house stands where the turnpike road enters the town. In 1845 the taking of the tolls on the gates leading into Kington was let for £800; this one fact shows the commercial advantages of being on the main road into mid-Wales.

This lower part of the town, now the town proper, is the new borough of pre-1267, 'Kington in the fields' as it was called then. The plan of the streets, whilst not unlike the grid of many medieval boroughs, could perhaps preserve the lay-out of an earlier open-field system as the name Furlong Lane may well imply.

Kington is sheltered on the west by Hergest Ridge and on the north by Bradnor Hill, almost 1,400 and 1,300 feet high respectively. Not only do they shelter the town but also provide it with plenty of open space; although much reduced today almost a quarter of the parish acreage in 1845 was common. In this respect as in some others Kington has much of the character of some of the Welsh market towns. A visit on market day would help to confirm this impression, especially at the time of the sheep sales or on a Saturday when the local football team is playing in the mid-Welsh League.

From Kington one of three ways can be taken to Pembridge. The first two leave the town past the old station towards Titley where

13.   Hereford Cathedral and the old bridge over the River Wye

the Herefordshire and Radnorshire Nature Trust have a reserve on a big pool to the north of the road. It is a wonderful spot for wild duck and geese especially at certain times of the year, but at any time there is a good collection of wild life. These pools are part of a series which were formed during the Ice Age and run from Titley through Staunton to the eastern side of Shobdon.

From Titley the more northerly route leads through a delightful, sheltered valley to Staunton-on-Arrow. It is lovely at any time of year, but at its best in late spring when the blossom is out. Staunton itself is a church, a school, a castle mound, a timber-framed manor house with a shell hood over the front door and a few cottages. Soft fruit of all sorts as well as apples and pears are grown here, while back in the Arrow valley below the village one is in good grassland with its Hereford cattle. The church and castle on the hill overlook the ford, the spot where the Roman road from Mortimer's Cross to Little Mountain and Clyro crossed the Arrow. Some years ago a Roman figure of the god Mercury, protector of travellers, was found here. There is no proof that it was not brought to this spot by a former vicar who was a great collector of historical objects, but it would be nice to think that the Romans erected it here to protect those crossing the ford.

The other road from Titley to the bridge below Staunton follows the river very closely. It crosses the Arrow at Hunton and then climbs to the high land overlooking the gorge and Mowley Wood. The road is little used today but the bends and climbs are worthwhile for the view over the valley which at one time must have been busy, for down by the river was a forge, no doubt the forerunner of those in Kington, using water power to drive its bellows and hammers. There were a number of these ironworks in the county and more will be written about them in another chapter. Like the Lugg and the Teme the Arrow has cut its way through a limestone gorge, not as spectacular as the others, for everything on this river is on a smaller scale, but an attractive part of its course, nevertheless. The road goes over a now disused level-crossing on the one-time branch-line from Kington to Presteigne and finally drops back again into the valley below the gorge rejoining the other road by the bridge at the Court of Noke. This is an early eighteenth-century brick house, beautiful in any setting, but here by the river and bridge it is a sight to enjoy, most of all in spring when the field and garden between house and road is a mass of daffodils.

The road to Pembridge keeps within sight of the river passing through the Row Ditch, a Dark Ages earthwork which runs across the valley for about two miles. It is a substantial vallum with a ditch on the westward side and may have been some sort of territorial boundary. This is good Hereford cattle country and good corn-growing land as well, the road passing some big, well-known farms, most of which had their own mills using the river as their source of power. Just north of the bridge which helps to give Pembridge its name are two timber-framed farms, one on each side of the road. Clearbrook, the bigger of the two, has three big dormers decorated with late cusping and brick-panelled chimneys of the last 20 years or so of the seventeenth century, an excellent example of the latest of the bigger timber-framed houses. And so the road reaches Pembridge, the end of the bridge.

From Staunton downstream the valley seems very broad for such a small river, but as the Lugg took over the old route of the Teme because its own course was blocked by glacial moraine so the Arrow took over the line of the Lugg. On its broad marshy valley was built the wartime aerodrome at Shobdon, now a repair and testing base for aircraft and the scene every year of two important air races.

Although the village of Shobdon is not strictly in the valley of the Arrow it is best considered with that river and is justly famous for its Strawberry Hill Gothic church. Lord Bateman, whose great house stood by the church until 1933, was a friend of Horace Walpole and under his influence the original Norman building was demolished in 1752 and a new one erected. The interior is painted white with a little light blue, the panels are stucco and the arches are typically Gothic ogee. All that remains of the early church is the Kilpeck-type font and the arches on the hill to the north, magnificently carved, but now unfortunately badly weathered after

200 years exposure to wind, rain and frost.

The Court was one of the houses to have its own gasworks very early. It was sited in a hollow well to the west of the house; one gets the impression that these early gas supplies were not altogether safe. Further west again on a hill is a game larder, dated 1803; it faces north and on each of its walls is a series of varying-sized hooks at different heights to take everything from deer to wood pigeon. It is a fascinating example of a type of building which disappeared with the coming of refrigeration. The great-crested grebe is found on the pool at Pearl Lake a short distance away.

The main road from Kington passes through Lyonshall, but before reaching the village there is first Penrhos Court, another big cruck house and, at the top of the hill, Offa's Dyke. As almost everywhere in Herefordshire it is not very impressive, possibly because it ran through the lands of the Earl of Hereford and was simply a boundary between English and Welsh custom and not as in many places a territorial boundary. The Earl had jurisdiction over much of modern Radnorshire. However, there is a good section of the dyke on Rushock Hill to the north of Kington and a stretch which can be well identified just south of Lyonshall. Overlooking the main road and adjoining the church are the scanty remains of yet another castle.

On the way to Pembridge a signpost to the north points to Marston. It is a hamlet of timber-framed houses interesting in that it once belonged to the nunnery of Limebrook and at the Dissolution there were eight tenements there, the rent varying from 16s 3d and a hen to 4d and a hen. Two of these farms were much bigger than the others. Today there are still two big timber-framed houses and six smaller ones. Some of these may have been rebuilt others partially so, but it would seem that here is a settlement almost fossilized in its pre-Dissolution state.

From whichever road Pembridge is entered it immediately catches the eye for it is one of the best timber-framed villages in the county. Strictly perhaps it should be called a town, for like Weobley and Wigmore it is a decayed medieval borough. In the centre just off the main road is the market-place; like many of those along the Marches it was roughly triangular in shape with a timber-framed market-hall. In this case the latter still stands with its seventeenth-century posts and mouldings. It is suggested that the notches in the posts were for holding planks on which wares for sale could be displayed, while on the east side of the hall are two stones which may well be 'nails' on which bargains were struck. A series of nails of this type is still to be seen outside the Corn Exchange in Bristol and in their use originated the expression 'Paying on the nail'. Around the market-place are the New Inn, an early seventeenth-century building, some black-and-white houses of varying dates from the fifteenth to the eighteenth century and the steps to the churchyard.

The striking sight as soon as one climbs these is the great pagoda-like bell-tower, a completely separate structure from the church. Before entering one should stop to look at the view northwards across the broad valley of the Arrow. There as background are the hills from Rushock—behind Kington to the west, Wapley, Shobdon Hill, Croft Ambrey to Bircher in the east. Depending on light and weather their mood changes from darkness and perhaps foreboding to one of sheer delight in the variety of greens and browns and purples. Perhaps the best time of all to stand in Pembridge churchyard is early in the morning when the sun is just lighting the tops of the trees on Wapley and Shobdon, or at sunset in autumn when the red hues of a setting sun light up the unforested slopes of Rushock and the trees cast long shadows in the valley below. The bell-tower is of a type found at Yarpole, a few miles away, at Brooklands in Kent and occasionally in Essex. Inside the stone, octagonal base are eight massive timbers rising to the height of the lower roof and reminding one of the stave churches of Norway, except that the construction is much heavier. It would be interesting to know why these two towers should have been built in north Herefordshire; where did the builder come from, whose influence was responsible for their design so different from anything else for nearly 200 miles? This is the finest and most remarkable of the county's detached towers. The church, like the belfry, is mainly of fourteenth-century work and is one of the bigger examples in the county befitting the borough status of Pembridge in the Middle Ages.

It would require a whole chapter to write about the houses of Pembridge, but it is a place to linger in and a delight for the photographer. There are probably more cruck houses here than in any other village in the county, perhaps than in any other village anywhere. In West Street as the road enters from Kington the first house on the left is a late seventeenth-century building with a big central feature on the front, a sort of timber-framed pediment, and very shallow jetties with carved pendants. The next two are both cruck houses each with an open hall and a cross-wing, probably dating fron the fifteenth century. All three houses are timber-framed though some of it is hidden today and all have roofs of local stone which fit well into this landscape. Throughout the village there is much of this work to see, a variety of types of jetty, some with good carved brackets, the beautifully carved bargeboards of the house on the main road below the church, the early sixteenth-century and close-set timber of The Greyhound, Duppa's almshouses built in 1661 at the top of Bridge Street and the very fine cruck house at the bottom. In East Street (what apt, simple street names), The Forge and Victoria Place are other medieval cruck houses and at the eastern end are Trafford's almshouses of 1686, each with its shaped doorhead, a typical feature of the Marches from here south and south-westwards.

For those with the time and the energy there is a footpath from Pembridge to Eardisland which is never more than a short distance from the river. A walk along it takes one through good meadowland, past a small copse and in sight and—perhaps just as important—sound of the river and its bird life.

The quicker and shorter way is to follow the main road which from just east of Kington as far as Eardisland runs along the ridge away from the possibility of flooding and away from what must have been before modern drainage a marshy, flat-bottomed valley.

Eardisland is a much photographed, picture-book village. Like

Kingsland and Monkland farther east it was part of the land of Lene, probably from the Welsh *lleoni* which means easily flooded. A bridge carries the main road over the river, these and the mill-leat winding around through the village as though wanting to spend as much time as they can in this lovely spot. The lawns by the river are so beautifully kept that a stranger wandering along the roads of Eardisland could be forgiven for thinking he was in a private park. To the south of the main road is the green with the church and castle mound beyond it. The former, like Pembridge, is largely of the fourteenth century with some of the rich decoration of that time. To the north is the manor house, timber-framed with a brick Queen Anne addition and in its garden a tall, square dovecote, gabled on each side. The old timber-framed school is right by the bridge and still retains a whipping-post at its northern end. The eyecatcher of this lovely village is the Staick House with its sandstone roof and swept valleys, its hall of the late fourteenth century, the west cross-wing of the sixteenth, the seventeenth-century addition to the east wing and its fine chimneys of *c.* 1600. Inside, the original beautifully carved roof is intact. The name Staick is said to be derived from 'stank', to dam water, a very likely meaning in this position.

The mill-leat used to work a mill in the village and goes on to Arrow Mill about a mile downstream. This was still worked occasionally in the early 1960s and is almost complete today with three sets of grindstones and a clover bossing mill in a tall timber-framed building, a cider-press and mill adjoining at one end and the traces of a hop-kiln at the other. Grain, clover, apples and hops were all processed in one complex. Between the mill and the road are the remains of a long-house in which the family had direct access from the parlour to the cattle in the byre without going outside.

The only remaining village on the Arrow is Monkland, mentioned above, with timber-framed houses and a cruck house showing its construction at the east end. The best approach from Eardisland is by means of the minor road which runs along the Moor Brook and takes the traveller across one of the comparatively few pieces of true common still remaining, surrounded by tiny cottages and with geese and cows wandering over it.

A tributary of the Arrow is Tippet's Brook. It must be mentioned, not only for the peace and beauty of the hamlets and farms and the minor roads which serve them, but for the timber-framed dovecote built in 1673 at Luntley Court with its 500 nesting boxes still inside. At Bidney is another very attractive black-and-white dovecote. The village of Dilwyn was a place where until recently it was not safe to stop, but now it has been by-passed and it is possible to wander round and look at the timber-framed houses and the church. This has a well-carved timber rood-screen and, as at Eardisland, the wealthy ball-flower decoration of the early fourteenth century is used, in this case on a tomb recess containing the effigy of a knight in chain armour. One little treasure is a quatrefoil panel of fourteenth-century stained glass with two angels swinging censers.

North of Dilwyn, through orchards of both apples and soft fruits, is Burton Court. Unlike the other houses mentioned in this chapter it is open to the public. The front is an early work of Sir Clough Williams Ellis, carried out in 1912 and visited again by the architect in 1974. The surprise is inside, for here survives a fourteenth-century open hall with its great arch-braced timber roof and cusped windbracing still complete. It is a magnificent example of the craftsmanship of 600 years ago.

Tippet's Brook joins the biggest of the Arrow's tributaries, the Stretford Brook, just above the bridge of the same name. This latter rises near Sarnesfield where lies buried John Abel who died in '1694 in 97th year of his age'. He was the great master builder whose work can still be seen in the county and his epitaph reads:

This craggy stone a covering is for an architect's bed,
That lofty building raised high, yet now lyes low his head,
His line and rule, so death concludes, are locked up in stone;
Build they who list or they who wist, for he can build no more.
His house of clay could hold no longer,
May Heaven's joy frame him a stronger.

Beneath are his compass, rule, bow-saw and square. The fine four-teenth-century roof of the church show the traditions which Abel was continuing as also do the still earlier inscribed stone coffin-lids which are preserved in the church. The Lion Inn is said to be so-named because it was built almost 100 years ago by a lion tamer.

Two miles down the valley is Weobley, the biggest of the county's 'decayed' medieval boroughs. To describe this feast of timber-framed building in any detail would need a chapter. Approached from Sarnesfield, Weobley is obvious as one looks down on it from the main road, but from Hereford one gets the strange impression of a spire stood in a field and it is only at the very entrance to the village that it is clear that this is not a magnificent folly. The church stands at one end, the castle at the other, the borough with its market-place and grid of streets between them. Even now, especially north-east of the church, it is possible to trace the earth bank which once surrounded the flourishing little town when the Welsh traded here for the renowned Weobley ale. MP for the town at one time was Colonel John Birch, the great Parliamentarian leader, who bought the Garnstone estate and settled here after the Restoration. Later the town became a 'pocket' borough of the Thynnes of Longleat and finally lost its representation in 1832.

There is so much to see in this, one of the great timber-framed villages of England. There are the fine, obvious crucks of Dairy Farm and the building behind the Red Lion, but the inn itself is probably 100 years older as are the so-called Manor House, a base-cruck building, and its neighbour in Bell Square. The old vicarage is a fourteenth-century house added to when married priests were allowed, 200 years later. On the western side of the main street facing the little garden which has replaced the old market-hall and other buildings is a shop built in the Wealden style. The only other known Wealden houses in the county are two which now form part of The Unicorn around the corner. They are distinctive in the way in which the hall roof projects forward to link up with that of the wing and probably date from *c.* 1400. Beyond the seventeenth-century Unicorn and around the next corner is the Old Grammar

School built in or just after 1658. It is now a dwelling-house, but look at the carving and moulded balusters of the porch and the little pendants from the window sills. Here as in all these Weobley houses the craftsmen gave of their best.

So far the church has hardly been mentioned, but in it are examples of work from the Norman period onwards. Its great fourteenth-century tower and spire proclaim Weobley and its wealth from afar. The Norman doorway, the rich fourteenth-century ball-flower ornament on the west doorway and north-east arch of the arcade, the fine roof with its scissors-braced trusses, the tombs and monuments in the chancel, including that of Colonel Birch, 1691, the medieval coffin-lid and the rather fine communion table of 1707 all make this church of more than usual interest.

But Weobley is not just one building, it is a living community of which its wonderful collection of houses is a part; it has to be savoured quietly and without hurry. It is a place to go back to again and again.

A short mile south-west of Weobley is the Ley. In many ways it is the finest sight of all the county's timber-framed buildings. Others are bigger, or have more decoration or are more picturesque, but this house of 1589 with its central block and two cross-wings, its fine stone and brick chimneys, and above all its silver grey, untreated timber, sums up in one building the workmanship, the proportions, the feeling for what is right that epitomizes the true craftsman. Herefordshire oak needs no treatment to preserve it, our modern black-and-white is a fashion of the last 200 years.

Further down the brook is Stretford, the site of a ford over the western branch of Watling Street from Kenchester to *Viriconium,* hence its name. It was the old centre of the hundred of that name and two bumps in the road may well indicate the circular enclosure where the moot used to meet. Like most of these small valleys that of the Stretford Brook floods easily in its lower reaches and from the trunk road a traveller could at times be excused for thinking there was a lake on the low land to the south. However, it soon clears.

The little church here, now redundant, but beautifully restored, is one of the few with a double nave and chancel, or if one wishes to express it another way an aisle and chancel aisle identical to the nave and chancel, but spanned by one fine sixteenth-century roof. Again there are fourteenth-century effigies.

South of Stretford is Birley, a scattered parish with a church and a few houses at its centre. The Norman font is a good example. Another road leads from Stretford across to Ivington and Brierley and for those who want to look out over the broad valley of the Arrow for its last few miles and its confluence with the Lugg this is the road to take. From the spur east of the hamlet of Brierley the view stretches across the meadows either side of the rivers to Leominster and beyond the town to Shobdon Hill, Bircher Common and High Vinalls, behind it to Clee Hill in Shropshire and the high land eastwards towards Bromyard. Below, almost on the river bank, but above flood level, is the brick Georgian farmhouse of Broadward Hall, its mellow bricks matching the soil from which they were made. Looking out over its broad acres it makes a fitting and peaceful finish to a river which has so many remains of castles of more restless days along its bank.

FIVE

The Lugg
and Leominster

Herefordshire rivers could be grouped by the number of market towns each helps to support. The Wye has seven, two of them, including Hereford itself, in this county and two on the boundary; the Lugg has two, one in the county and one just out of it; the Arrow has one; the Monnow has one which it shares with the Wye and just out of Herefordshire.

All these rivers have their sources in the mountains of Wales, running down to Herefordshire through picturesque, steep-sided valleys full of history, rich in botanical interest and fascinating to the geologist. As they flow across the rich red sandstone soils of this county they slow down, meander and water the farms in their valleys. Finally all unite in the Wye.

For hundreds, probably thousands, of years men have followed these rivers from the hills to the plain; from the land where living was sometimes difficult to richer, better land farther east. At one period it was raiding for cattle or sheep, for a long time now it has been a more peaceful penetration. Many a Radnorshire farmer has worked and saved on a hill farm and then moved to the richer land of Herefordshire. A glance at the electoral roll of any west Herefordshire parish will show the Radnorshire surnames in the local farms. It is a gentle, peaceful migration which still continues.

A minor invasion in the other direction occurs year after year in the fishing seasons. Trout are plentiful, salmon find their way back up the rivers and there are plenty of lesser fish. The angler from the industrial Midlands or from London comes out in coaches on Sundays or stays at one of the local inns and pursues his contemplative sport in the peace of these valleys.

The Lugg has its source near Llangunllo on the edge of the Clun Forest, flows past the seventeenth-century house at Monaughty, past the battlefield at Pilleth where Glyndwr defeated Mortimer in 1402 and so to Presteigne, one-time county town of Radnorshire. The northern outskirts of this little town are actually in Herefordshire just as, on the Wye, Hay spills over from Brecon.

East of Presteigne the road to Leominster runs across a flat stretch of land from the outskirts of the town itself to Byton. This is the bed of a glacial lake formed when the Wye valley glacier dammed the course of the Lugg during the Ice Age some 30–60,000 years ago. When the ice receded the terminal moraine remained to block the old course of the river which then found its way out at the lowest point on the rim of the lake.

The best impression of the latter is obtained from Byton churchyard, built on the moraine and affording a fine view across the basin to the hills of Radnor Forest and the wooded Wapley Hill to the south, crowned by an Iron Age hill-fort. Built into the wall of the nineteenth-century church is a lintel bearing a carving of the Agnus Dei from the Norman building which once stood here.

The river leaves the basin in the north-east corner where over the last 30,000 years or more it has cut a way through the Silurian limestone to form an impressive gorge. No road runs through this, but for the walker there is a rewarding path alongside the river past Kinsham Mill through the depths of the gorge to Covenhope, and those with plenty of time can follow it on to Aymestrey. Almost all the way to the south of the river are forested hills, the 'league of wood' which was entered under Shobdon at the time of Domesday.

Woodland, pasture and limestone cliffs leave an impression of quietness and peace. It was at Kinsham Court, overlooking the gorge, that Byron once stayed and Florence Nightingale's family lived, while much later Sir John Arkwright here wrote the hymn 'O valiant hearts, who to your glory came'. This peaceful spot with its church across the park must have seemed a long way from the battlefields of France.

Before reaching Aymestrey the river flows under Lyepole Bridge. It was here that the writer in his early days in the county found two lads poaching. It was a lovely, lazy midsummer afternoon and if one must break the law what better way could there be to do it? Anyway, they probably didn't catch anything, but just enjoyed the afternoon, and the river, and the thrill of taking a risk.

Above them, hidden in the forest is the almost perfect motte of the Norman castle of Lye. Strangely the Lugg has few castles along its Herefordshire section. Here, in a land of castles this river has failed to get its fair share. Even Leominster seems never to have had one. Near Presteigne on a small tributary is Stapleton Castle, now crowned by a ruined seventeenth-century house, and a little further downstream is Coombe, a very small motte. These with Lye and Kingsland are the Lugg's rather meagre share of the county's castles. Even if Croft is included it is still a small number.

Leaving the main valley at Lyepole Bridge is the Covenhope valley, now dry because of glacial action, but thousands of years ago the Lugg ran this way. It is the first real area of corn-growing on the river and from here down to the water-meadows close to the confluence are fields of grain, wheat or barley or sometimes a mixture of both, muncorn as the farmers of years gone by called it. The change in colour and texture of this landscape is a delight to watch through the round of the year. Rich red-brown in autumn after ploughing followed by a fresh green among the brown as the young new crop comes through after the autumn sowing; sometimes this becomes white with snow for a while. Then spring when the green becomes fresher and stronger, slowly, almost imperceptibly, changing to a pale gold as it grows and ripens, until that final period before the harvest when for a short time it is a rich, deep golden colour. Harvest in and there are the evening fires as the stubble is burnt, and then, sometimes the very next day, the rich red-brown of the freshly ploughed earth. The cycle has started again.

Aymestrey with its timber-framed cottages, church, mill, eighteenth-century court and bridge over the Lugg is a typical Herefordshire village. However, it is remembered for its one-time curate, Rev. T. T. Lewis, who married the daughter from the Court against her parent's wishes and who also played a prominent part in geological investigation. It is partly as a result of his efforts that the county learned society, the Woolhope Club, was founded and that Aymestrey limestone became known to geologists all over the world. The bridge dating from 1795 was one of a number built by a Kingsland engineer, John Gethin, who did much for the road system of the county.

The church is worth a visit just to look at the early sixteenth-century woodwork of the rood-screen and the parclose screens at the east end of each aisle. Linenfold panelling, running-vine ornament and the trefoiled and cinquefoiled arches with sub-cusped heads all help to show the skill of the medieval woodcarver and to delight us today. The heavy twelfth-century Norman piers look too big and out of proportion in this church. Are they from that short period when a monastery was started here before moving to Wigmore and which apparently gave the name Monk's Bowling Green to the levelled area behind The Crown?

One of the battles which helped to change English history was fought on the banks of the Lugg at Mortimer's Cross. Here on Candlemas Day, 1461, Edward, the young Duke of York, whose mother's ancestral home was at Wigmore, four miles away, gave battle to the Lancastrian army led by Owen Tudor. It was a bitter, frosty day and the refraction of light by the ice particles high up in the atmosphere caused the opposing armies to see the phenomenon of a parhelion, or three suns, a symbol still portrayed along with the red and white roses of Lancaster and York on the sign of the local inn. Edward's men took the parhelion as a symbol of good fortune and after the Lancastrian leaders had refused York's challenge to single combat a day-long battle followed ending in complete victory for the young Duke who a month later was crowned Edward IV. He had used his local knowledge in defeating his opponents and his right wing seems to have trapped Pembroke's men on the opposing left and massacred them in the Kinsham gorge.

At Mortimer's Cross today is one of the few remaining working water-mills of the county now in the care of the Department of the Environment. Half-an-hour spent here watching the custodian demonstrate the grinding of grain into flour gives an excellent impression of the use made of these rivers. The Lugg and its tributary the Arrow provided between them the power for at least 50 mills, a number of which were still working until well after the Second World War. In some cases their machinery is still fairly complete today. Iron wheels came into use about 70 years ago but a few were still using wooden wheels until the end. For those who have not previously heard and felt the thudding of a mill until the whole building shakes, it is an exciting and rewarding experience.

One of the local leaders who supported Edward at Mortimer's Cross was Croft of Croft Castle, a fifteenth-century fortified manor house about two miles east of the battlefield. Unfortunately the western gate is no longer in use; thus the castle cannot now be approached by the chestnut avenue. Even so these fine trees can be seen from the terrace of the house, which belongs to the National Trust. It is still lived in by members of the Croft family which has been here since before the Norman Conquest except for a break from 1746 to 1923 when they bought back the estate. Those who visit the house will find that the Johnnes family gothicized it at the end of the eighteenth century. As a result it has become a pleasing mixture of medieval and romantic gothic. The top 'storey' is simply a façade added to impress, but so skilfully designed that it deceives many visitors. The family tie-up with Downton will be dealt with when that house is written about later.

The outstanding feature of the little church is the altar tomb with the effigies of Sir Richard Croft, 1509, and Eleanor (Cornewall), his wife, with a standing canopy over the heads of the figures. The west end of this tomb has canopied recesses containing figures of St Anthony, St Roche, St Margaret and St Sitha with their respective symbols. Along the south side and alternating with the saints on the

14. Detached fourteenth-century belfry at Pembridge, internally of stave construction

west end are cinquefoiled and crocketted recesses with male figures in them.

From Mortimer's Cross the Lugg leaves the hilly part of its course and flows through flat, rich farmland. No longer are there forests and limestone, but in their place fields of grain or cattle and red sandstone soil. This change of rock and use also marks the change from the more sparsely populated areas to the bigger villages of black-and-white timber-framed houses, dependent on farming.

The first of these is Kingsland. To its north and west is the great west field over which the battle of Mortimer's Cross was fought. The hedge patterns today still show the line of the open-field strips of the pre-enclosure period. Here on the plain the English feudal farming methods prevailed and elsewhere in the county a few strips are still held on the common-field system.

Kingsland village at first gives the impression of being a mixture of stone, brick and timber-framed houses, but a closer look shows that they are almost all black-and-white with false fronts added in the late eighteenth and early nineteenth centuries to give the village a Georgian appearance. No doubt neighbour tried to outdo neighbour in having the most modern front. The landlord of the old Bell Inn was unlucky. As the building stands on a corner the front and one end had to be bricked.

The church is well worth a visit. Unlike many churches it is almost completely of one build. The early fourteenth-century craftsmen have left us a spacious, dignified building of which the chief glory is perhaps the crown-post roof, an unusual feature in this part of England and no doubt erected by a band of travelling carpenters trained in the methods of eastern England. Even the remaining medieval glass in the chancel windows has survived from the same century. The Volka Chapel adjoining the porch is a puzzling but attractive feature. It may have been a chantry chapel for the occupant of the stone coffin which still lies against its south wall. Close by the church is a big castle mound and beyond it the old vicarage, a beautiful Queen Anne building.

Near the village is a farm with an iron aqueduct constructed

15.   Dilwyn Church, arcades *c.* 1300, screen and roof fifteenth-century

across the Lugg to carry the mill-leat, the water then being led across the fields by an irrigation channel to a farmyard from where it was used to flush out a drainage ditch. It finally rejoins the river some two miles from where it left it. This careful use of water is a good example of the ingenuity and foresight of the local farmers.

Eyton is one of those little hamlets which can be so easily missed and yet the picture of an area is not complete without them. The road runs across a low-lying common by the Lugg, unfenced and with cattle regarding it as their right-of-way as much as the motorists'. In spring it is a mass of buttercups. On the edge of this common as the hill slopes up to the hamlet is the aptly-named Marsh, a deserted farmhouse. The great hall of the medieval house is now used as a barn but its beautifully carved roof is still intact. The central truss with its arched-brace and foiled openings above, the two tiers of cusped wind-braces and even the traces of the spere truss at the service-end are still there.

Across the road on slightly higher ground out of reach of the floods is Eyton Court, with its timber-framed cross-wing catching the eye much more readily than the earlier Marsh.

Still farther up the hill is the little church with its late fifteenth-century rood-screen. This, with its coved, panelled loft and its double band of carved foliage, reminds one yet again that every corner of the county has its own peculiar interest.

Leominster, the county's second biggest town and only surviving borough until the local government reorganization of 1974, does not impress when entered from south, east or west, probably because it lies on the flat, marshy meeting place of the Lugg and its tributaries the Pinsley and the Kenwater. Only from the north on the modern Ludlow road is there a hint of the town's importance and interest as one gets a glimpse of the priory church above the river. The names of three of the town's wards, Lower, Middle and Upper Marsh give some indication of the low-lying easily flooded area around the confluence of the streams.

It is probably because of this that early man avoided the present site of the town and it is not until the Dark Ages that there is any hint of a settlement here.

There has been some doubt about the origins of the town but modern research favours the theory that a religious community was founded here by Merewalh, a Saxon Prince of the Magonsaete and brother-in-law of Ethelred, *c.* 660. It served as the ecclesiastical centre of the Magonsaete until Hereford Cathedral was founded some time later. About 680 a mixed community was founded at Much Wenlock and it seems that the church at Leominster may have been of a similar nature. It is possible that if Leominster had grown more quickly it might well have become the cathedral city. It is more centrally situated in the diocese than either Hereford or Much Wenlock. Leofric, Earl of Mercia apparently re-endowed the community in the eleventh century. The old name *Llanllieni* almost certainly means the church in the land of Lene, the name given to the area including Leominster, Kingsland, Monkland and Eardisland.

In the *Anglo-Saxon Chronicle* we read '1046. In this year earl Swein marched into Wales. . . . When he was on his homeward way, he had the abbess of Leominster fetched to him, and kept her as long as he pleased, and then let her go home'. It seems that after this the community declined and was dissolved. After the Conquest its great local estates were divided.

In 1123 Henry I gave Leominster to the Abbey of Reading and soon after began the rebuilding giving us much of the fine church we have today. The nave and north aisle of the twelfth-century priory church are still in use but the choir, transepts and Lady Chapel were destroyed after the Reformation. The parishioners' nave, the south nave, was built in the thirteenth century for use as a parish church and apparently replaced the Norman south aisle. In the early fourteenth century the south aisle was added. This and the Norman west door catch the eye perhaps more than the other features of this fine building, because its windows all contain the ball-flower ornament. This decoration is typical of the period and is found mainly in the midlands and south-west of England. It is a sign of wealth in the builder and gives some idea of the prosperity of an area in the period *c.* 1300 and just after. The west doorway responds are carved with interlaced work and with figures of doves, snakes, lions and one of men reaping. Inside on the north impost is the carving of a man and lion usually said to be Samson and the Lion, but it may be that the sculptor had heard the legend of the founding of the seventh-century community when Merewalh dreamt that an anchorite had news for him. A hermit had dreamt that in a certain spot a lion had fed out of his hand. Next day they met and the king, whose nickname was Lion, realized that his church must be built on the spot seen in the dream.

A secular relic now preserved in the priory is the ducking stool, last fully used in 1809, there not being enough water to duck the last person condemned to it in 1813. It was used to punish scolds and sellers of adulterated foods.

The late afternoon or early evening is the time to visit the priory if possible, for then the rich red of the local sandstone shows at its best.

In spite of the stone of the great church Leominster is a black-and-white town. A short distance from the churchyard is The Grange, now the offices of the District Council. It is one of Herefordshire's best timber-framed buildings having been built in 1633 by John Abel as a town hall, standing at the top of Broad Street. It was offered for sale in 1853, was bought by John Arkwright of Hampton Court and re-erected on its present site. It seems ironical that the borough should have bought it back for its original use. Basically of the same square-panelled construction as most Herefordshire seventeenth-century timber-framing it also has Renaissance ornament in some profusion as well as ogee-shaped braces, a comparatively rare feature. Originally it had an open ground floor which was used as a butter market. Ross and Ledbury halls still have their open ground floor today.

This market-hall is the finest remaining example of the work of John Abel, 1577-1674, who seems to have been the leading Herefordshire craftsman of the first half of the seventeenth century. Besides the hall at Leominster he built those at Brecon (1624) and Kington (1654), also the stone grammar school (1625) at the latter

town and the ceiling of Abbey Dore Church (1633). During the
siege of Hereford in 1645 he constructed a powder mill and for this
was given the title of the King's Carpenter. Other work attributed
to him includes the once magnificent town hall at Hereford
(1618-20), destroyed 1862, those at Weobley (destroyed about 1860)
and Ledbury, the hall of the Butchers' Guild, Hereford (1621), the
screen at Abbey Dore, the Unicorn at Weobley, buildings at
Weobley (destroyed in the 1930s), Orleton and Pembridge and the
church ceiling at Vowchurch. There is no documentary proof of his
building any of these, but the screen at Abbey Dore bears the same
inscription as the Leominster Market Hall. Unfortunately the Brecon
and Kington halls have been destroyed, but the former was not as
ornate as Abel's later work. He is said to have engraved his own
monument which can still be seen in Sarnesfield churchyard.

The timber-framed wealth of Leominster can be seen in Corn
Square, in Draper's Lane and School Lane leading from it and in
High Street. It is worth walking along the alleyways between
Draper's Lane and High Street just to see the mouldings of the
bressumers of the jettying. Look above the shop windows. In this
way is seen the surviving timber-framing. One shop in High Street
has three really grotesque carved heads as brackets. Broad Street and
its continuation Bridge Street have their share of good timber-
framing.

Two other streets need looking at—Church Street and Etnam
Street. The former, leading from the one-time site of the market-hall
to the priory, is mainly eighteenth- and nineteenth-century and
shows how well the Queen Anne and Georgian builders used the
brick made from the Herefordshire marls.

In Church Street is the Forbury Chapel, now an auctioneer's hall.
It was built in the precincts of the priory in 1282 and it is worth
going in to a sale preview to see the fine hammerbeam and
scissor-trussed roof, probably a unique combination, dating from
c. 1500. It has been in turn chapel, town hall, school and lawyer's
office before being used for its present purpose.

Etnam Street is also a good Georgian street with a number of timber-framed buildings still remaining. In it is the town museum, an entirely local effort, housed in a hall built in 1855 as a mission room for navvies working on the construction of the railway. At the western end is the Royal Oak. This late eighteenth-century hotel incorporates an earlier timber-framed building, but on its first floor is an assembly room running the length of the building and two storeys in height. An even more elaborate assembly room until recently did duty as an agricultural engineers' store at the Black Lion works in Broad-Street. This also was once a hotel and one wonders which of these two fine rooms was the Tory gathering place and which the Whig.

Enough has been said to show that Leominster was a wealthy little town. It would be easy to assume that it was from the rich farmlands around producing grain and cattle. It was, but even more important was wool, the 'Leominster ore'. The local breed of sheep, the Ryeland, produced this wool, which, if we believe Michael Drayton, the seventeenth-century poet, 'with the silkworm's web for smallness doth compare'. Isaak Walton commented that 'certain fields near Leominster, a town in Herefordshire, are observed to make the sheep that graze upon them more fat than the next and also to bear finer wool', while Robert Herrick wrote of 'a bank of moss more soft than the finest Lemster Ore'. In the early days of the industrial revolution it seemed that Leominster might become a minor centre of the woollen industry and here Daniel Bourn invented the carding machine in 1748. He had already introduced cotton manufacture into Leominster, but his factory was burnt down in 1754 and not rebuilt.

In an area of many cattle leather is bound to be important and Leominster was no exception, the main tanneries being in the Lower and Middle Marsh areas on the banks of the Lugg and Pinsley.

For a short time Leominster had a canal. It had been intended to go from Kington to Leominster and on to Stourport but only the section from Leominster to Mamble collieries was ever completed, the first coal carried on it reaching Leominster in 1796.

Leominster has produced few men of note, but one, John Scarlett

Davies, 1804-45, did become a well-known artist. His main love was architectural painting, but his enormous output includes portraits, engravings, lithographs, pen-and-ink work as well as water-colours and oils.

Today Leominster is a thriving market town with a new industrial estate and continues its long tradition of providing a centre for the commercial and social life of north Herefordshire. Perhaps if the Lugg and Pinsley had been more swift-flowing it would have become a centre of wool manufacture like Stroud, but here on the plain instead of in a steep-sided valley the water-wheels did not get the power to drive the big textile mills.

The Lugg has never been a really navigable river. An act was passed in 1674 for making the Lugg and Wye navigable and there were further acts up to as late as 1809. A basin was built at Eaton Bridge and the venture was successful enough for Leominster Priory bells to be taken to Chepstow and back for recasting in 1750. However, flooding made the use of the river difficult and sometimes dangerous though it was possible to write in the eighteenth century that 'Both the navigations are, however, of great use to the county'.

Beyond Leominster, especially after the Lugg has been joined by the Arrow, the wealth of this river valley shows in the type and quality of the buildings. Foremost among these is Hampton Court. This important fifteenth-century house is built around a courtyard with a gate-tower in one wall and the great hall opposite it across the yard. At one corner is the medieval chapel. Most of the house has remained unaltered externally in spite of some early nineteenth-century additions. Altogether it is a fine example of a defended, medieval house, making a splendid sight above the Lugg from the main Leominster to Ledbury road. It is surrounded by good farmland and behind it rises Dinmore (*Dyn mawr*—great hill) Hill. It was built about 1435 by Sir Roland Lenthall who had fought at Agincourt and was Yeoman of the Robes to Henry IV. It passed by marriage to the Cornewall family and was bought by the Coningsbys whose descendants sold it to Richard Arkwright, son of the inventor of the spinning jenny, early in the nineteenth century. It is his descendants who now live at Kinsham Court, mentioned above.

Until the Great War it had a deer park to the north of the road but then the fences were allowed to decay, the deer escaped and their descendants can be seen today in the Queen's Wood on Dinmore. The fallow deer is a shy creature, but even if the animals themselves are not seen the patient walker will find the tracks of deer and badger on the paths through the wood. This area was part of the manor of Marden and was purchased by Richard Arkwright in 1810. Most of its fine oak and beech woods were felled during the Great War, and the land became covered with scrub, bracken and young trees and seemed to be getting out of control. However, in 1935 it was acquired as a memorial to the Silver Jubilee of George V. The area nearest the main road has been developed as an arboretum with specimens of some hundreds of trees from all over the world. Beyond this is the Queen's View where from the edge of the escarpment can be seen a panorama of Herefordshire from the Malvern Hills in the east to the Black Mountains in the west.

It is often said that the modern craftsman cannot equal the work of his medieval predecessors. Perhaps those who visit the Preceptory of the Knights of St John of Jerusalem at Dinmore will change their minds. Here in a peaceful and beautiful setting is the chapel and part of the conventual buildings of the knights, restored in the present century and containing some fine modern wood carving.

The village of Bodenham is beautifully situated around its green. From here came the Devereux family, later Viscounts Hereford, and at the southern end of the village is a house once known as Devereux Court. It is an impressive timber-framed house with a fine solar fireplace in the cross-wing which dates from the fourteenth century. It must have been a very important house, probably the seat of the family. The other houses around the green and the church are the later two-room plan type probably built in the seventeenth century and there are one or two bigger houses of eighteenth-century date but still timber-framed.

In the church is an early fourteenth-century effigy of a woman with coif, wimple and long cloak, her right hand on the figure of a small child. It is a very unusual monument to somebody whose name we do not know; could she have been the mistress of Devereux Court? Both doorways have the rich ball-flower ornament of the same period.

The same decoration occurs in the main entrance to Broadfield Court, a fine fourteenth-century stone house in this area of timber-framing, standing on the hill well to the north of the village.

Very close to the village are the extensively worked sand-pits, a result of outwash of fine gravel and sand from the ice-sheet which covered the hills towards Bromyard.

The area from Bodenham southward along the Lugg is flat, easily flooded in times of heavy rain but with much good black-and-white timber-framing. Sutton St Michael, Sutton St Nicholas, Marden, Preston Wynne are all good examples of timber-framed villages.

In the nave of Marden Church near the west wall is a well. It seems that after Ethelbert's murder, possibly at Sutton Walls, his body was brought here and buried. Legend has it that when it was moved to Hereford, *c.* 1030, water gushed out of the ground at this spot. Thus we have St Ethelbert's Well in Marden Church. The east end is a fine fourteenth-century apse, an uncommon feature in Herefordshire.

Another story connected with the church concerns a bell which fell into the river when the belfry was being built and was carried to the river bottom by a mermaid. Twelve heifers were harnessed to it by yokes made from yew and mountain ash. The bell was drawn out in complete silence, for the mermaid was asleep inside. However, the driver boasted rather too soon that the bell had been landed, the mermaid awoke and dashed back into the river taking the bell with her. It has not been seen since, though it is reported that occasionally it can be heard ringing.

At Amberley Court is an almost unaltered timber-framed house probably built soon after 1400. It is of that rare type of construction known as base-cruck. Of the nine Herefordshire examples three, Eaton, Amberley and Preston Wynne, are in the Lugg valley. At Eaton, just south of Leominster, lived the Hakluyt family one of whom wrote about the voyages of the Elizabethan sailors, while Amberley was the home of the Lingens, a prosperous county family. These houses with their roofs of carved timbers and their spere truss, the entry into the great hall, were the homes of the rising gentry, some of whom fought at Agincourt, represented their county in Parliament and played their part in the Wars of the Roses. An excellent example of them is open to the public at Lower Brockhampton, but there is more about that area elsewhere in this book.

Sutton Walls, high above Sutton St Nicholas and Sutton St Michael, is a great hill-fort occupied in Iron Age times and through the Roman period. Giraldus Cambrensis calls it *Villa Australis* in his account of the murder of Ethelbert by King Offa. Leland refers to 'a stone castle' here. It seems possible that this site may have been occupied into the Dark Ages.

Lying west of the main Leominster-Hereford road below the southern slopes of Dinmore Wellington is apt to be overlooked, yet it is one of the county's bigger and more interesting villages. Almost every period of timber-framed construction is represented in it and it is rewarding to walk the length of the village looking at each building in turn. From the early Georgian brick Bridge Inn the street first passes Bridge Farm. It is worth stopping and looking across the bridge at it. Black-and-white, square panelled with a wing at each end it is typically Herefordshire set in its big farmyard with the brick and timber-framed outbuildings, the cider-mill, the stream forming the boundary on two sides and orchards on the others. Inside in the far wing, the eastern end of the house, is a solar on the first floor with its great stone fireplace built about 1400 and a decorated plaster ceiling inserted some 200 years later. In the centre is the remains of a massive, arched-brace truss which once showed off the owner's wealth to his visitors, while the far end of the west wing of lighter framing is a later seventeenth-century addition to the house, a hop-kiln.

The church, with its good Norman tower still surviving, again shows the woodcarver at work. The porch roof is one of the best in a county with many good porches and it rests on stonework again displaying the ball-flower of the fourteenth century. The quatrefoiled north aisle roof with its pierced cusping and beautifully carved cusp points is of the same period while the nave roof, constructed probably over a hundred years later, has big carved square bosses. The church is a wonderful example of the art of the craftsman in wood and stone.

At the west end of the churchyard is the Old Parsonage, part of which dates from the fourteenth century, presumably the house of the celibate priest of medieval times. Post-Reformation additions were made on the south side, probably to help accommodate the family of a married vicar. However, in 1636 he and his family got a new timber-framed house, the Old Vicarage, farther up the street on the opposite side. Before reaching it two other buildings catch the eye, an octagonal brick dovecote with a pyramidal roof and lantern, the whole dating from the early eighteenth century, and a long timber-framed barn with its heavy wattling still exposed. In houses wattling was narrower and intended to be covered by daub and plaster; in barns this wide wattling was in itself the wall material and has matured to a silvery grey or brown according to the time of day and the state of the light.

So this street goes on for three-quarters of a mile with a variety of timber-framing and some good brick made from Herefordshire marls. The road off to the north across the Wellington Brook has a number of late timber-framed houses probably of the eighteenth century using much thinner timber than the earlier ones.

The Wellington Brook should be followed farther west to Canon Pyon and to King's Pyon and Wormsley. The first of these has a number of late timber-framed houses, a church with good carved misericords and the Great House, Georgian brick and bow-windows completely encasing an earlier timber-framed dwelling. Above the village, up a steep hill is Westhope Common. It is one of the great commons of the county and the view from the top is magnificent in every direction. Come up here on a fine day when you have plenty of time and just wander, for besides the great open space at the top there is a maze of unsurfaced lanes with little houses, some stone, some timber-framed, some brick, typical haphazard, unplanned, commons development, many of them no doubt built on the old custom of getting a hearth and a shelter erected in one night. At the end of the tarmac road is Birches Knoll, a rare example of flat sandstone slabs pinned to a timber-frame, a type of construction which will be noticed again in the south-west of the county.

King's Pyon will be remembered for the eighteenth-century timber-framed dovecote and the magnificently carved church roof erected 400 years earlier. It has deeply cusped wind-braces and heavily-foiled struts and like the Renaissance dovecote at Buttas, a mile down a lane from the village, is a wonderful example of the woodcarver's art.

Wormsley is a few scattered houses, a redundant church and the site of an Augustinian priory. The siting of both, the former high up and open, the latter in the valley surrounded by and approached through woods is splendid, the one announcing that here is a place of worship, the other secluded, a place of retreat from the world. In the churchyard are two fine table tombs to Richard Payne Knight and Thomas Andrew Knight, grandsons of the ironmaster, and both born at Wormsley Grange. Richard became known internationally as an antiquary and collector, Thomas as a horticulturalist, but both were brought back to this peaceful resting place at the end of their lives. Why are their tombs north-south instead of the normal east-west?

Above the Lugg east of Pipe and Lyde Church on the main Hereford road stands a brick house. Near it is a stone where the sheriff and javelin men used to meet the judge to escort him into Hereford when he came on circuit. From the accounts which have come down to us it appears to have been a convivial occasion.

The early fourteenth-century, slender octagonal spire is a good landmark to lead one to Withington across the marshy countryside. The village is well-known for its tiles which have been made here since at least 1848 and have been used in many cathedrals, Windsor Castle and even Armidale Cathedral in Australia. Felton, Ullingswick, Moreton Jeffries, Ocle Pychard and Westhide lie in the small tributary valleys flowing across good mainly low-lying farmland with wealthy farms typical of this part of the county.

The Lugg's last few miles are through water-meadows passing the biggest of all this river's mills just below the bridge carrying the main Hereford-Worcester road. Like most of the mills it was rebuilt in the eighteenth and nineteenth centuries. These were important buildings in the economic life of the county and were constantly remodelled and rebuilt to keep pace with changing milling methods and demands on their capacity to deal with increasing crops. Thus they are not always picturesque in appearance but like most good, functional buildings they have clean pleasing lines. Below Lugwardine on the east bank is Tidnor Forge, with traces of the moorings for barges which once followed the iron trade up the Lugg. Later it became a corn-mill, but now is just another quiet, secluded building with memories of a busy past.

Above the village of Mordiford is Sufton, a square, late eighteenth-century house lived in by the Hereford family who have held the manor of Mordiford from medieval times, when their rent was a pair of gold spurs to the King of England whenever he should ride over Mordiford Bridge. Perhaps he did not come that way often enough, for in 1304 the rent was changed to a pair of gilt spurs annually to the value of sixpence. By 1387 the value had risen to half-a-mark, three shillings and fourpence, or in modern English money about 17 pence.

The Lugg joins the Wye just below the village, the last bridge over it carrying the road from Hereford to Gloucester being one of the finest on the whole course of the river. It is partly fourteenth-century, partly sixteenth-, and makes a good foreground in the setting of church, bridge and vicarage with the hills of the Woolhope Dome behind. They are a handsome group when viewed from the west bank, a fitting finish to the Lugg.

SIX

Hereford

The word city conjures up all sorts of pictures of smoke and industry and crowds and endless streets of industrial revolution houses. This is not at all what Hereford is like for it is a mixture of ancient defended city, cathedral city, administrative centre, market town, industrial town and tourist centre. Perhaps it is a market town above all, but it would not be Hereford if it did not have all these facets.

The See of Hereford was founded in 676 and according to Giraldus Cambrensis writing over 500 years later a stone cathedral was built by Offa, probably in 792. Certainly a stone cathedral was built by Bishop Athelstan c. 1020, but this was badly damaged by the armies of Gruffydd and Aelfgar in 1055 and a completely new building seems to have been started c. 1080. Nothing visible remains today of the pre-Conquest cathedral, but every century from the twelfth to the twentieth shows some influence on the present building.

Externally, the exuberant use of the early fourteenth-century ball-flower ornament on the great central tower is bound to catch the eye. The colour of the red sandstone seems to vary with the light and in the evening glows in the setting sun.

Internally, the massive piers of the Norman nave, the delicate Early English work of the Lady Chapel, the beautiful chantry chapel of Bishop Stanbury with its fan vaulting, the ball-flower over some of the tomb recesses, the monumental effigies and brasses all have their interest and attract people according to their own particular likes and dislikes. The whole makes up a typical, medieval English cathedral which has gone on changing and adapting to the needs of the times, and should be looked at as an entity.

The cathedral benefited from the shrines of two saints, Ethelbert and Thomas de Cantilupe. The former was the young king of East Anglia who was murdered in 793, possibly at Sutton Walls, on the orders of Offa, King of Mercia, or of his wife Queen Quendreda. It seems that his body was first buried at Marden and then at Hereford where miracles were performed at the tomb. Ethelbert, the young celibate king became a martyr and a saint. Thomas de Cantilupe was bishop of Hereford from 1274 to 1282 when he died in Tuscany on his way home from Rome. His bones were brought to Hereford, some 400 miracles were reported to have been wrought at his tomb and a commission was appointed to enquire into them as a result of which he was canonized by Pope John XXII 25 years after his death, the last English saint in the calendar of the pre-Reformation church.

One of the great treasures of the cathedral is the Mappa Mundi, world map, dating from *c.* 1300, the only surviving example of its size and character from that period. The cathedral chained library of 1,444 books housed over the north transept is the largest such collection in the world, the earliest manuscript in it dating back to the seventh century.

In addition to these beautifully illuminated manuscripts similar to the famous Book of Kells in Dublin and the early Northumbrian manuscripts in Durham there are preserved here a magnificent Limoges reliquary of the thirteenth century and other relics.

The cathedral close is almost part of the town's Broad Street, but between the cathedral and the river lie the cloisters of the Vicars Choral approached by a passage with a magnificently carved roof. The cloister is surrounded by houses, originally 27 in number, each of which housed one of the Vicars Choral when they moved here *c.* 1475 after complaining that it was dangerous to come into the cathedral at night from their earlier hall in Castle Street because of attacks by 'evil-doers'. Today only a few yards from the busy streets of the city this is a peaceful little haven of quietness.

To the west of these cloisters is the Bishop's Palace, probably the earliest surviving timber-framed building in the country, though now encased entirely in brick. Its great piers and arches dating from *c.* 1180 still survive, showing the size and quality of the oaks in the bishop's forests.

As a defended city the story of Hereford goes back about as far as that of the cathedral. There was a Roman town at Kenchester a few miles west on which the system of Roman roads centred, but at present there is no certain evidence of settlement in Hereford until the Dark Ages, though there appears to have been a ford across the Wye in Roman times below the present site of the bishop's palace. Excavations in various parts of the city have shown that there was a ditch and rampart around part of it from at least about the 9th century, but there is evidence of Anglo-Saxon settlement some 200 years or more before this. The medieval walls and 17 bastions were erected in the thirteenth century along the immediately pre-Conquest line enclosing an area much bigger than the early defences which on the north had run along the line of the present East Street and West Street, where the ditch outside them still causes problems to builders.

Inside this earth-and-timber rampart, in the south-east corner was built a castle, one of the first Norman castles in England, in the years before 1055 when it was sacked by the same Welsh army that burned the cathedral. Harold Godwinson rebuilt this and also probably had built the first earthwork along the line of the northern section of the present city walls before making his retaliatory invasion of Wales in 1063.

The walls and their six gates continued in use until the Civil War of the seventeenth century, the last of the gateways being demolished in 1798. Today the best impression of the walls and ramparts is obtained by a walk over the Wye bridge and around the ring road. The great motte of the castle remains as a public park, the ornamental pool being part of the old moat.

The area between the cathedral and the castle down Quay Street and by St Ethelbert's well is now a quiet, residential district well worth a walk past timber-framed and mellow brick houses with quite unexpectedly a pair of seventeenth-century brick gazebos in a garden. The walk along the river bank on the edge of the old castle defences gives good views of the river and the Row Ditch, perhaps part of the original defence system, on the southern bank and of the General Hospital, built in 1783. The very name Quay Street reminds one that this was a river port and that the city has depended for its existence on trade. The best place to see this is at the market in Newmarket Street. A great cattle and sheep market like this, is a fascinating thing to watch. The stranger can enjoy the atmosphere of this to his heart's content, but it is to be hoped that he will also realize that what is new and interesting to him is an essential part of the way of life of the farming community of this rural county and all who depend on it. Here at different times of the year are the lamb sales, the great sheep sales of the autumn and the sales of the white-faced, red Hereford cattle which attract buyers from all over the world.

Back in the centre of the town is a jostle of shops and people and traffic, but High Town and Eign Gate are now pedestrian precincts; so one is free there from the motor car. Off High Town is the Butter Market where produce from the local area is displayed for sale. Here are stalls selling fruit, flowers, butter, cheese, dressed poultry and here too is a collection of true Herefordshire characters.

At the time of the second visitation of the Black Death to Hereford, from August 1361 to May 1362, the market was moved to the White Cross on the northern outskirts of the city. This beautiful piece of work bears the arms of the then bishop, Lewis Charleton, and may have been used as a preaching cross as well. At the earlier outbreak of the plague in 1349 the remains of St Thomas Cantilupe had been carried in procession through the streets as protection against the dreaded disease. This belief in the saint seems to have been effective, for Hereford itself escaped quite lightly though some of the county suffered badly.

The medieval street names tell us something of the activities of the city. Bakehouse Lane (1436), the Butchery (1310), Corveseresrewe (Shoemakers' Row) (1386), Mercerierewe (1321),

Sadelwryhtstrete (1317), tell their own story as do Frenchman Street (1225), Jewry Lane (1554), Fryers Lane (1436), Oldescolestrete (1397) and Quakers Lane (1757). Golden Alley, probably not really very 'golden', connected the Butchery to Cooken Row by the Old House, but what went on in Synestrete (13th century)?

The earlier market-hall stood in the centre of the new pedestrian precinct in High Town. It was one of the great timber-framed buildings of Europe, built possibly by John Abel, but was demolished in 1862. Today it can only be admired in old prints and in the model in the Old House. This latter building stands at the east end of High Town, a carefully preserved, early seventeenth-century timber-framed house, the only survivor of a row of houses which once stood here. It is used as a museum by the city authorities and in it one can get some idea of life 350 years ago. Outside are the highly ornate, carved bargeboards protecting the ends of the purlins, the longitudinal roof members, the pentice roofs, the pendants on the jettying. Inside is furniture of the early seventeenth century, some murals, the carved oak overmantel and stone fireplace of the great chamber and a more or less fully equipped kitchen of the period.

The city is fortunate in having three other buildings with civic connections still surviving and as they are all in typical Hereford streets it is worth mentioning each in turn. Perhaps Hereford's most picturesque street today is Church Street leading from High Town to the cathedral. It used to be known as Cabbage Lane though the earliest recorded form of the word is Cabocheslone in the thirteenth century. The glimpse of the cathedral, the variety of buildings and shops make this a street to be walked along slowly. At the north end nearest the cathedral is a timber-framed shop and in an upstairs room is a seventeenth-century decorated plaster ceiling with the old city coat-of-arms on the gable wall, for a former mayor once lived here. Along East Street from the crossing with Church Street is the Booth Hall Hotel. This was once the meeting place of the city justices and administrators, the site having been acquired for that purpose in 1292. The dining-hall of the hotel still has its very finely carved timber roof with alternate tie-beams and stub-tie beam archbraced collar trusses. Along the sides of the roof are deeply cusped wind-braces in the form of great quatrefoils. This is a fine piece of craftsmanship. The third building with civil connections is the Mansion House in Widemarsh Street, built in 1697 by Dr William Brewster and now a shop. Outside the heavily decorated cornice catches the eye; inside the fine ceilings and fireplaces show the change in taste and outlook from the times of the Booth Hall and the Church Street house.

Hereford has had a mayor since 1382 and a charter since 1189. Under local government reorganization it has been given the authority to keep its mayor and the council still meets in the Town Hall built in 1904, while close by stands Smirke's Shire Hall of 1819.

A number of Hereford's shops have interesting timber work or plaster-work inside and beneath some of them are fine cellars. One of these which is accessible is that at the tavern on the corner where Bewell Street joins Widemarsh Street. Here one can sit and enjoy a drink in a carved, stone-vaulted cellar. As with the cathedral and the churches this cellar shows that the medieval stonemason was able to produce just as fine work as the woodcarver. As in any medieval and Tudor town much of interest is hidden away behind later façades and modern shop fronts, but enough still exists to give some idea of what these streets looked like three and four hundred years ago.

Two of the city's five medieval churches still stand. All Saints at the top of Broad Street contains the second of Hereford's chained libraries. In 1715 Dr Brewster, who built the Mansion House, left his important collection of books to the Bodleian and St John's College, Oxford, and to All Saints Church. Two hundred and eighty-five books on 'Divinity, Morality and History' came to the church and to these have been added a few more; so that today there are 326 books here. In the mid-nineteenth century a churchwarden sold this almost unique collection to a dealer for £100, but fortunately the Dean of Windsor and the Bishop heard of it before the books left the country and ordered them to be restored to All Saints.

They were just in time, for books and chains had already reached London. Thus Hereford still has the two largest of England's six chained libraries.

The hammer-beam roof is a form of construction rare in the county, but that of All Saints is a good example and worth studying from a seat in the pews. Here also is the ball-flower ornament once again, this time on the piscina. St Peter's, which stands near the Old House, celebrated its ninth centenary in 1974 having been founded as a collegiate church in 1074. Its status was short-lived, however, for in 1101 it became a priory church dependent on the Abbey of St Peter at Gloucester and then in 1131 an ordinary parish church. Hugh de Lacy had become bishop of Hereford, finished the building of the cathedral and demoted the churches of St Peter and St Guthlac in the market-place and castle respectively.

As the stranger walks around the city he is bound to notice some of its 18 groups of almshouses. The most famous is undoubtedly Coningsby's Hospital in Widemarsh Street, founded in 1614 on the site of the Hostelry and Chapel of the Knights of St John of Jerusalem. The new foundation had 12 houses for poor soldiers, mariners or serving men, a chapel and hall and infirmary. One of the servitors, an ex-soldier, was to be the corporal of Coningsby's Company of Old Servitors and the head of the hospital. Their uniform was to be a peaked cap and a long scarlet cloak. It has been suggested that this is the origin of the Chelsea Pensioners' very similar dress, the thought being that Nell Gwynne, a Hereford girl, persuaded Charles II to adopt it when he founded his great hospital at Chelsea. Incidentally a plaque still marks her birthplace in Gwynne Street at the west end of the cathedral, the street now having taken the name of its most famous (or infamous?) resident. By one of those strange tricks of fate her grandson, Lord James Beauclerk, came to Hereford as bishop for 41 years from 1746, living in the palace against whose western courtyard wall was the birthplace of his grandmother.

The most picturesque of the almshouses is the group in Berrington Street, Aubrey's Almshouses, founded in 1630. It is timber-framed with the ovolo moulding of the period prominent in its doorways and windows and little quarter-circle decorative timbers in the panels.

Situated in the central Marches close to the Welsh border Hereford has always been a civil and ecclesiastical adminstrative centre as well as one for trade and industry. The Shire Hall, the County Gaol as well as, later, the County Hospital and the various further and higher educational institutions were naturally built in the city. The College of Education, high up above the city, has the distinction of being the first teachers' training college in the country to have been founded by a local education authority. This was in 1904 before which it had been a boarding school; it is a typical Victorian gothic building with all the frills of the different pointed styles incorporated into it in the way our forefathers of 100 years ago loved. Unfortunately it is now scheduled to close in 1978.

In 1953 an event happened which was to make a difference to Hereford: a big nickel alloy factory was established on Holmer Road, opposite the racecourse. For the first time in peacetime a major industrial enterprise had been established in the city with all that this means for employment, housing and servicing. There are other industries in the city, but the one which is typically Herefordshire is, of course, the making of cider. In the cathedral library is a fifteenth-century bible which instead of the more usual 'strong drink' says, 'he schal not drinke wyn ne sider', a fifteenth-century reference to the county's drink which has been made world famous by one of Herefordshire's cider-making families, the Bulmers, who first made the drink in 1887 at the Rectory at Credenhill.

It is strange to think of Hereford as a shipbuilding town, but there was a yard opposite the Castle Green from which a brig of 170 tons was launched in 1823. The steamship *Paul Pry* was built there in 1827.

Hereford has then its various facets as a cathedral city, defended city, market town, administrative centre and industrial town. As a centre in this way it is bound also to become a focus for sporting activities, entertainment and learning. The football team hit the headlines in 1972 as FA Cup 'giant killers' and to prove that this was no mere run of good luck, having got themselves elected into the football league, gained promotion from the Fourth Division in their first season and in 1976 got into the Second Division. The race-course has been functioning since 1771, perhaps earlier, and race dates have been highlights on the social calendar year by year. As early as 1839 the building of a grandstand was discussed, but whether it was ever actually constructed at that time is not known, though there was one in existence by 1865 when Grandstand Road was given its name.

Canoeing and rowing on the river can at least provide a pleasant spectacle for the less energetic who sit in comfort on the river banks. The rise in popularity of canoeing over the last 20 years has been considerable and a number of centres have become established along the Wye. The writer was slightly puzzled at meeting two young ladies who had been awarded certificates as inspectors of the banks of the River Wye; it was the means by which an enterprising youth-hostel warden attempted to persuade them to steer a more accurate course.

As for cricket, perhaps its quality in Hereford is summed up by the fact that in the mid-nineteenth century an All-England XI used to play 22 men of Herefordshire on Widemarsh Common, a custom revived by the great W. G. Grace, but unfortunately allowed to lapse again.

Bowls has been played in Hereford since at least 1533 when some people were prosecuted for playing 'le boullynge'. They may have played on the green which is still used behind the Bowling Green Inn in Bewell Street. It was certainly in existence in 1697, but is claimed to have been there since 1484. In either case it is a very old green and probably vies with that at Southampton in claiming to be the oldest in the country.

Tom Spring, boxing champion of all England in 1823-4 was for a time landlord of the Booth Hall.

The great musical event in the Hereford calendar is the Three Choirs Festival which every third year takes its turn to come to

Hereford. It is probably the oldest European music festival, having started *c.* 1720 when the choirs of Gloucester, Hereford and Worcester Cathedrals met together to make music. The famous name connected with the festival is Sir Edward Elgar, who first came to it as a violinist in 1878 and lived to conduct at it in 1933. Every year his *Dream of Gerontius* is part of the last night's performance. For eight years, 1904-12, he lived in the city during which time he produced some of his greatest work. He was too busy to become mayor of Hereford when invited to do so in 1905. John Bull, the reputed composer of the National Anthem, was organist at the cathedral for four years from 1582.

Drama played a prominent part in the life of the city until the closing of the Kemble Theatre in 1962. It seems possible at the time of writing that the Garrick, closed in 1940, may re-open. This theatre was named after the greatest name in the drama world to come out of Hereford, David Garrick, who was born in 1716 in an inn which stood on the corner of Widemarsh Street and Maylord Street, the site being today marked by a plaque. The name Kemble itself also has associations with the city, for Roger Kemble was born in Hereford in 1721 and both he and his daughter Sarah (Siddons) acted here.

One of Hereford's sons who was for long forgotten was Thomas Traherne. He was born *c.* 1637, the son of a shoemaker in the city, but seems to have been brought up from an early age by a relative who kept an inn and was twice mayor. He graduated from Brasenose, Oxford in 1656 and was for nine years vicar of Credenhill, before going to London where he died at the early age of 38.

A surprising sight which sometimes greets one in Hereford is a steam locomotive, for here for some years has been the home of *King George V* and other engines of that now almost-past era. They are looked after by the 6000 Locomotive Association which works in conjunction with Bulmer's publicity film and exhibition which are shown in converted Pullman coaches.

In Broad Street almost opposite the west front of the cathedral is a high Victorian building with some wonderfully strange creatures in stone crawling along its parapet. It is the museum and library, built in 1873 as a gift of James Rankin. The county's learned society, 'The Woolhope Naturalists' Field Club' was founded in 1851 for the practical study in all branches of the natural history and archaeology of Herefordshire. It soon felt that a museum was needed to house the collection of fossils, natural history specimens, historical and archaeological objects being brought together by its members. Sir James Rankin offered to have such a museum built and to combine it with a library and a room for meetings of the club and to give the building when finished to the City Corporation. This was done and all three parts of the original intention are still carried on in it, for the Woolhope Club holds its meetings in the Woolhope Room on eight or nine occasions each winter. It still runs six field days each summer and of recent years has held a week's visit to another county each year. With a membership of nearly 900 it really is continuing its founders' intentions, probably in a way they could hardly imagine. Every year its *Transactions* find their way to universities and learned societies all over the world. There is one change its early members would not have imagined: women were admitted to membership in 1954 and since then there have been four women presidents.

To one of its past distinguished members, Alfred Watkins, goes the distinction of inventing the light meter, the Bee Meter, as he called it. In those days, it sold for 2s 6d. Watkins is also well-known for his book *The Old Straight Track* in which he propounds the theory of leys, lines from one ancient monument to another, not usually looked on with favour by archaeologists, but undergoing a certain resurgence of popularity today.

The club's early fungus forays hit the headlines in the national papers of the time. The great Mycophagoi festival was held in 1874, members collecting edible fungi and then repairing to one of the city's leading hotels to cook them and eat them. These forays were an annual event from 1868-92.

Also in Broad Street is the local headquarters of the Women's Institutes. They and the Young Farmers' Clubs, one of the most successful of all youth organizations, are an important part of village life. If you feel like scoffing at rural society go to a YFC debate or public-speaking contest or general knowledge quiz or the annual drama and entertainment festivals or talk to a WI gathering and answer its questions; you may be surprised. All this is part of a Herefordshire community.

At the top of Aylestone Hill to the north-east of the city is a pleasant garden in which are the costume and art galleries of the museum. Here in this quiet garden one can sit and enjoy a view over Hereford, the towers of the cathedral, the spires of All Saints and St Peter's, the circle of hills from Dinedor around to the Black Mountains and Hay Bluff, the roads and the railway lines leading into the city and the Wye valley wandering away to the west and to the south. Without going outside its boundaries, from here there is almost a bird's-eye view of Hereford.

It was below this spot that in December 1645 Colonel Birch's men hid in readiness for the ruse which was to result in the fall of Hereford to the Parliamentarians. The Colonel hired six men and dressed them as labourers, who with a constable were to enter the town on the pretext of having work to do. In the remains of St Guthlac's, where the omnibus station is now situated, he hid 150 men with firelocks while he himself and a body of men lay in a hollow up Aylestone Hill. At daybreak on the frosty morning of 18 December 1645, the constable and labourers went up to Bysters Gate when the drawbridge was let down, and while the guards were examining the warrant, first the men with firelocks and then the soldiers from Aylestone Hill overcame them, rushed inside, and took the city without bloodshed.

The best approach to Hereford is probably from the south from the Ross direction; as the descent from the hill at Callow is made so the city appears with the cathedral dominating the scene. A convenient lay-by makes it possible to stop and enjoy this view with the city in the foreground and the long line of Dinmore behind it and much farther away to the northeast the Clee Hills in Shropshire. An even better view is that from Dinedor Hill, the great Iron Age camp to the east of the main Ross road. From here John Price in 1796 described the view as 'over the river Wye, which meanders with great beauty through a most luxuriant vale, finely blended with woods, corn fields and pasture grounds'. The description still applies today and the scene above is encircled by the Malverns on the east, the Clee Hills, Dinmore Hill, Credenhill Camp, the hills behind Moccas to Merbach in the west.

On the road out of the town to Ledbury is an inn, The Cock of Tupsley, with a sign of a shire horse which must at first seem a little odd, but in fact 'cock' was a name given to some big horses, probably shires, which were kept here to help pull loads up the steep hill from the Lugg valley below.

At this point one is already away from the city and overlooking open country. It is here and at Holmer, Huntington and Rotherwas that one realizes that Hereford is a market town serving a big rural area and that it quickly melts into the countryside it serves.

Holmer, just north of the Roman road which is an effective boundary to the city on the north, has a church with a detached, partly timber-framed tower. The chancel roof has both hammer-beams and collar-beams with tracery above both, a most unusually elaborate roof of a type not normally found in Herefordshire. The churchyard cross has the early fourteenth-century ball-flower decoration on its base.

Huntington with its church and court in the trees by the Eign Brook, although officially in the city, is a quiet little Herefordshire hamlet. It is in some ways typical of the atmosphere of this market-town city that within its actual boundaries should be one of the farming communities on which it depends.

If one wants to take away a picture of Hereford, mental or photographic, one of the best places to do so is from the new Wye Bridge looking back towards the city over the river, to the old bridge and its reflections in the water, to the cathedral and the castle mound beyond, to the spire of All Saints. Here in one picture is Hereford's story. Whether it be when the river is in flood or in quieter times when there is rowing from the boathouse just below, canoeing and men and boys fishing this is one of the views to remember of Hereford.

SEVEN

East to the Malverns

This is a chapter of contrasts for from Hereford to Mordiford the flat flood-plain of the Wye and the Lugg is completely different from the scenery further east. On a slight rise in the ground is Hampton Bishop, an ecclesiastical manor with some very attractive houses, including crucks, along the loop off the main road. In the church are the remains of a stone reredos, a rare fifteenth-century feature. Down the lane behind the Bunch of Carrots below the river bank is a small empty house which must be among the last fully timber-framed dwellings to have been built in Herefordshire.

The road along the east bank of the Wye from Mordiford to Ross is squeezed for most of its way between the river and a great block of Silurian limestone, the Woolhope Dome. Like the similar formation in the north of the county around Aymestrey and Wigmore it was laid down over 400 million years ago and is a delight for the walker and for the motorist who does not mind narrow roads and steep hills, for no main road crosses it; they go round it. There is a maze of these lanes and many a driver has been temporarily lost in the ups and downs and ins and outs of this beautiful, quiet piece of Herefordshire.

The area, with its succession of steep scarps and gentle dips, the alternating limestones and shales, with its fossils and its variety of flora and fauna, has attracted the naturalists and geologists for many years and in 1851 gave its name to the county's learned society, the Woolhope Naturalists' Field Club, which still flourishes. On the western side approached by a steep hill from Mordiford is Haugh Wood partly belonging to the National Trust. Walks are laid out in the wood to enable the naturalist to study his chosen plants or birds, but equally to give enjoyment to the non-specialist who just wishes to have a quiet walk through the wood.

It was down the steep slope above Mordiford that in 1811 the Pentaloe Brook, swollen by 'a tremendous storm of Thunder, Lightning, Wind, and Rain', swept hundreds of tons of rock and carried away a barn, cider-mill and cottage in which four people were drowned.

Between Haugh Wood and the village of Woolhope is Broadmoor Common, a stretch of comparatively level, rough pasture surrounded by late timber-framed houses probably built during the eighteenth century on land enclosed from the common. Their framing is thin, almost fragile looking, compared with the heavy timber used in earlier houses.

Five minor roads meet in Woolhope village, a collection of stone houses round the parish church which is worth a visit for its collection of thirteenth- and fourteenth-century coffin-lids, one of them under a cusped and crocketted canopy enriched with the early fourteenth-century ball-flower ornament.

Along the lanes east of the village is the Wonder, the site of a landslip in 1575. Various accounts of this so-called 'earthquake' have survived. About 20 acres of land seem to have slid down the hill as a result of a layer of rock slipping over the clay below it in much the same manner as more recent examples along the Dorset coast. There were apparently no injuries or deaths but the chapel at Kynaston, 'sheep-folds, hedges and trees' were carried before the hill as it 'walked'. The chapel bell was unearthed by the plough some 250 years later and is now in Homme House at Much Marcle. Earthquakes were recorded in Hereford itself in 1661 and as recently as 1975, as well as other tremors from time to time along a fault line which runs from the Malverns to the Neath Basin.

South of Woolhope along the lanes is Sollers Hope, a church and a farmyard in their own secluded valley down a track across the fields. Church, farmhouse and barn make one of those natural, beautifully balanced groupings that seem to just happen without conscious planning; here stone, timber and brick combine harmoniously. But the glory of Sollers Hope is the brick chimney-stack on the Court Farm. It must date from the second quarter of the sixteenth century, is crow-stepped above eaves level and surmounted by two octagonal shafts with trefoil-headed panels on the bases and topped by moulded concave-sided caps. Such a chimney is a rare sight anywhere in the country.

From Sollers Hope a lane takes the traveller up Ridge Hill, the southern end of Marcle Hill. On the limestone ridge is the Iron Age hill-fort of Oldbury Camp and here opens out a view across the rich farmland of the valley of the Leadon to Ledbury and the Malvern Hills. This is the great hop-growing area of the county, the poles of the hop-yards and the cowls of the hop-kilns being much in evidence as one looks over the valley from the high land above. It is an area of wealthy farmhouses and farm buildings, some as early as the fourteenth century, others dating from all the periods of farming prosperity ever since, the 'great rebuild' of 1570-1640, the 'Golden Age' of 1850-75, and the recent rebuild of 1950-75.

The dominant village, right on the Gloucestershire border, is Much Marcle. Like so many others in the county it is a place in which to linger, to savour it unhurriedly like good wine. The church, with its central tower, probably follows the Norman plan, but it is remarkable for its effigies. Two of this good collection stand out. One is to Blanche (Mortimer) wife of Sir Peter Grandison, 1347. It is on an altar tomb with an elaborate canopy. The whole is beautifully carved, but the effigy itself is what really matters. Here lies Blanche in her tight-sleeved gown, wimple, close-fitting headdress and long veil, with her rosary in her hand, dog at her feet and train hanging down over the end of the tomb. The whole is strikingly beautiful and realistic as she lies with her eyes closed and her lips slightly parted. It is an effigy not easily forgotten. The other is probably of Walter de Helyon, a franklin or wealthy freeholder, who is in civil costume of a close-fitting, buttoned jerkin, tippet with rolled collar, hip belt, short sword and wallet. It is a wooden effigy, probably dating from the third quarter of the fourteenth century. So rare are these wooden likenesses that recently he was taken to London for exhibition as an example of a franklin.

One other piece of carving in the church must not go unnoticed. The eastern respond of the south arcade is carved with foliage sprouting from the mouth of a man's head, the green man of medieval mythology. However, take a close look at him: on this pagan symbol the craftsman has carved a cross on a chain around the neck. Was he taking an each-way bet on another world?

In the churchyard is a giant yew some 30 feet in girth. Its trunk is split and inside is a seat for seven people. A cobbled causeway leads past a timber-framed house back to the road across which is the fine Queen Anne rectory built in 1703, now renamed Phillips House. It is one of a number of houses in Much Marcle which are worthy of notice, not all because they are big. Just south of the church is the Bower, a tiny, single-cell house of cruck construction with a thatched roof. When it was built in the sixteenth century the sleeping accommodation was probably on a platform the full width of the house and about three-quarters of its length.

Close to the church is Homme House, partly early Tudor, partly Queen Anne and partly late Georgian, the home of the Kyrles whose fine tombs are in the north chancel chapel of the church. Hellens lies down a long drive and stands on the site of the house in which Walter de Helyon lived. He was succeeded by his son-in-law Richard Walwyn and it was this family which built the Jacobean brick house which stands here today. It is very much worth a visit and also gives an opportunity to see a cider-press and a cider-mill *in situ* in one of the out-buildings. Away from the village along the road to Putley and Aylton is Hall Court, a fine timber-framed house built in 1608. It stands in a garden by the roadside and opposite is a mound which was partially excavated in 1974 and was no doubt the site of the earlier house.

Cider is still made at a factory near Much Marcle, one of the two remaining small establishments still at work in the county. Whether in a works like this or on a farm it is a fascinating process to watch. Not many farmers make their own cider today, but where they do the apples are first crushed in a circular stone 'mill' or trough by a stone 'runner' pulled by a horse. The pulp is put into 'hairs', a form of sack, and pressed by screwing down baulks of timber. The process has a language of its own.

This road takes the traveller past farms with their hop-kilns, through hop-yards and orchards, good arable land and yet never far from the sight of herds of cows. A lovely story is told how during the Second World War some bombs were dropped in a field near here and a bull which objected to having his peace disturbed in this way refused to allow the air-raid wardens across a field to the scene of the bombing. He probably saved them from serious injury, for, until some little time later while they were still going round by the lane, neither he nor they knew there was a delayed-action bomb among those dropped.

Aylton, like Sollers Hope, is a collection of church, Court Farm and barn standing away, slightly aloof, from the other houses of the hamlet. The tiny church with its equally tiny bell turret could well be in the middle of Radnorshire or in the Black Mountains from its style and appearance. It is Norman, but its fifteenth-century screen alone would make it of interest to a visitor. It is worth stopping here and reflecting that in this modest building our predecessors worshipped their Lord with all the colour and ceremony and simplicity of faith of the medieval church just as in the much more magnificent surroundings of Much Marcle. And here, for all its humbleness the woodcarver worked his screen and 200 years later in 1654 another craftsman turned the balusters of the porch. The church may be small, but for cathedral-like proportions look across the farmyard at the great six-bay cruck barn built perhaps about the same time as the screen was carved.

Ledbury is the market town and centre for this south-eastern area, but instead of taking the direct route it is perhaps better to go first to the head of the river Leadon and follow the valley down to its main town.

16. *above* Buckenhill Manor near Bromyard; 17. *below* Holme Lacy house, built *c.* 1675 for Viscount Scudamore

The road to Bosbury joins the main road at The Trumpet Inn and then goes off to the north-east through Munsley. To the enthusiast the church is interesting because of the early Norman herringbone work in the chancel and the lettered stone built into the south wall of the nave which may well be Anglo-Saxon.

There is no 'best place' to see the valley of the Leadon. The whole of its width from Marcle Hill to the ridge east of Ledbury is delightful at any time of the year. Its attractions are the orchards in spring, the cornfields in August, the colours of the autumn leaves in October, but the changes from pale green in spring to the red of the freshly-ploughed soil in autumn provide a background which is an important part of the picture. In this general scene the rapid growth of the hop-bines from ground level to some 12 feet in the course of a few months and their sudden disappearance at the harvest help to add further change. The black-and-white timber-framed houses fit into this landscape and become an integral part of the picture providing a sudden but not too violent contrast to nature's own colours.

Evesbatch is at the head of the Leadon but it is more easily seen with the villages of the Frome. Bosbury is the most important Herefordshire village on the river and at one time may well have tried to rival Ledbury, for it had some pretensions to borough status, but never succeeded. It was one of the great manors of the bishops of Hereford, whilst the Knights Templar also had considerable possessions in the parish. The village street is one to be walked along slowly enjoying the houses from The Crown and Bridge House at one end to The Dog, strangely enough apparently never a public house, at the other. It is basically a black-and-white village, but there are one or two very pleasant brick houses as well. Both Bridge House and The Dog were properties from which the rent helped to support the Free Grammar School which stands in the churchyard. It was founded in 1540 and the two houses seem to date from about that time. The school is no longer used for that purpose, but its black-and-white western side, rebuilt in the seventeenth century, still makes a picturesque corner east of the church. The Dog bears

18. Rowlstone Church in the Black Mountains

evidence of having been an open hall and its great moulded beam as a canopy over the master's high seat is still *in situ*.

The church is a fine Transitional Norman building with the unusual feature of a detached bell-tower just south of the main building and a little later in date. In the church the carved, late fifteenth-century rood-screen again shows the work of the craftsmen in wood. However, stone is more important here for there is the early sixteenth-century fan vaulting of the Morton Chapel, a rare feature in the county, and the Harford tombs. There are two of these each with sarcophagus, effigy and elaborate canopy. That in the south wall is to John Harford who died in 1559 and is signed with the date 1573 by John Gildon of Hereford, one of the leading west midlands craftsmen of the period. It is a finely carved, restrained piece of early Renaissance design of a quality which could well be found in a wealthy town church. Opposite is the tomb of Richard Harford and Martha his wife. Richard died in 1579. Superficially this tomb is similar to the other, but Gildon probably carved only the effigies, sarcophagus and inner arch. The monument seems to have been finished by two other local carvers probably used to working in wood rather than in stone. They have left us, instead of fluted Corinthian columns, Eve on one side and Adam on the other with a face so long that he looks as though he may have just been caught 'streaking'. In each spandrel is a green man with foliage sprouting from his mouth. The Harford family lived at the house which is now The Crown Inn where there is a finely panelled room of 1571.

North of the church is Old Court Farm, the earlier manor house of the bishops of Hereford. The gatehouse with its major and minor gateways dates from the fourteenth century. The house itself, looking very much an eighteenth-century farmhouse, still contains much of the timber work of the fifteenth-century manor house in its roof and in one room downstairs.

By the side of the lane south to Ledbury is Pegs Farm, another of the big fourteenth-century timber-framed base-cruck houses with an added early seventeenth-century parlour wing with small, square panels in contrast with the big irregular ones of the main part of the building. This farm is in the parish of Wellington Heath which gets its name from the north-western part of a Silurian limestone area and here again are the late timber-framed enclosure cottages, some of them very small indeed, less than 20 feet long, but with two rooms on each of ground and first floors, and quite probably dating from the second half of the eighteenth century.

From the north Ledbury is entered through orchards, past the Hop Marketing Board building and a preserves factory, in themselves evidence of the local farming. Across the fields is the many-arched brick railway viaduct, an unusual sight in this county and reminiscent of Cornwall and Devon except that there it would be stone.

The road is known as the Homend, the 'Hom' part being a common place-name in this area, going back to very early Saxon times, meaning a 'bend in a river' and later being used for low flat land near a river. It is sometimes spelt 'ham' and it is difficult to tell 'ham' or 'hom', 'near a river', from 'ham', 'a village'.

Like Bosbury Ledbury was a bishop's manor and like Ross and Bromyard became a borough. The *Red Book* of the bishops is a survey of the episcopal estates at the end of the thirteenth century when Ledbury with 282 tenants was the biggest of the five boroughs listed. The two outside Herefordshire were Prestbury in Gloucestershire and Bishop's Castle in Shropshire. At Ledbury were 33 *seldae* or stalls and it is not until almost a century later that there is reference to *schopa,* shops.

Little of this very early period remains in the town today, most of the timber-framed buildings dating from the sixteenth and seventeenth centuries. The obvious centre is the timber-framed market-hall built in 1633. Notice that on its south gable and west side the framing is of the decorative herringbone type while on the parts not so easily seen from the street it is square panelled. Even civic authorities put their best face outwards to 'keep up with the Joneses'.

Opposite is the long range of St Katherine's Hospital or almshouses, rebuilt in the nineteenth century with its fourteenth-century chapel and hall still at the south end. The hall is sometimes open and should be visited for a sight of the magnificent original roof which dates from *c.* 1340. Perhaps the ideal time is on the day of the weekly WI market when the visitor also sees something of the produce and colour of the surrounding area.

Legend has it that the hospital was founded by St Katherine (Audley) who was related to Edward II. The story is told by Wordsworth in one of the least inspired of his sonnets that Katherine heard the bells of Ledbury pealing without ringers and resolved to stay here with her faithful attendant Mabel who is still remembered in Mabel's Furlong at the south end of the town. In fact the hospital was founded in 1232 over 80 years before the local saint, in 1313, granted her possessions at Ledbury to James de Ferrers and settled as a recluse.

Until the nineteenth century two rows of buildings stretched up the main street, one of them continuing the line of the market-hall, the other between it and St Katherine's. One of the houses from the eastern row, Butchers' Row, has been rebuilt at the end of one of the long burgage plots which stretch back behind the houses, some of them for over 100 yards. These plots must have been both yard and garden to the fine houses fronting the street, but in the late eighteenth century and the early nineteenth small houses were built on them creating slums comparable to those in the big industrial cities. In the Homend there is still evidence of this on the north side where a plate by a doorway reads 'Nos 41-67'; this entrance led to the appropriately named Smoke Alley. It is still possible to follow one or two of these alleyways along the edge of the plots and one leads up between two shops on the east side of the High Street through into Worcester Road giving a glimpse of a rebuilt house from the Butchers' Row on the way.

At the main crossroads at the top of the High Street stands Ledbury Park, one of the few really big timber-framed houses in the county. It was built at the end of the sixteenth century and is probably on the site of the former bishop's palace. Here, as in some other houses in Ledbury, some of the main windows have small lights on either side at the top rather like little wings. It is an East

Midlands and East Anglian fashion which seems to have just managed to penetrate into Herefordshire in this south-eastern corner.

Timber-framing in much variety is in evidence in every street in Ledbury, from a cruck gable in the Homend to the elaborate Renaissance work on The Feathers and in The Talbot, but at each end of the town is an unexpected and pleasant piece of Regency planning. Off the South End is a small but complete little development of stuccoed villas while near the station at the northern entrance is some early nineteenth-century gothic revival.

The street which everybody who visits Ledbury seems to remember is Church Lane with its timber-framed buildings at each end, cobbled surface, hanging flower baskets and the church at the far end. Here is a heavily framed building dating from *c.* 1540. Its original use is uncertain, but during the eighteenth and nineteenth centuries it was used as the grammar school. Beyond it is a square brick house with its chimneys at the corners and a doorway which looks as though it could have been designed by Gibbs himself.

Looking down on the churchyard are Upper Hall and Lower Hall, the one-time homes of the portioners for, like Bromyard and Ross, Ledbury was a big parish served originally by a team of priests. In these three important bishop's manors the Saxon minster system seems to have lived on. Today after the Paul Report it seems the church is returning again to this old system.

The parish church of St Michael and All Angels is worthy of this wealthy little medieval borough. As in many Herefordshire churches the great period of building was during the early fourteenth century, but, as the west front shows, there had been a great Norman church here long before that. The *tour de force* is the outer north chapel, no doubt built by the same masons as the south aisle at Leominster. There are windows on three sides, these and the doorway being enriched with ball-flower ornament while the cusp points are carved as leaves. It is a wonderful piece of medieval craftsmanship, perhaps one of the most satisfying in the county. The timber work of the roofs of the aisles, 15 bays in the north and 11 in the south with the curved braces to the collars and the curved wind-braces shows the fifteenth-century craftsman in wood at his best.

There is a fine collection of monuments, floor slabs and brasses. Three should perhaps be looked at in some detail. In the chancel is that to Edward Skynner, 1631, and his wife Elizabeth, kneeling figures with the body of their young daughter lying between them, their other five sons and five daughters kneeling on the front of the base. It is a simple Renaissance monument, but look at Mrs Skynner's hat. It would grace any Easter parade. The others are in the north chapel and the outer north chapel respectively. The former is reminiscent of that of Blanche Mortimer at Much Marcle. Here on a semi-canopied altar tomb surrounded by 18 shields, many with heraldic devices, lies a sister of Grymbald Pauncefot who married a Carew. She is in wimple, head fillet and long gown draped over the side of the tomb, evidence of the growing naturalism of the age of Chaucer. The third monument is the recumbent effigy of a priest in his mass vestments dating from the late thirteenth century, and for the portrayal of feeling in his face it could be regarded as the finest monument in the church. Also in the north chapel lies Edward Moulton Barrett, Mr Barrett of Wimpole Street, father of Elizabeth Barrett Browning.

Ledbury is associated with two other famous poets, William Wordsworth, and the late poet laureate, John Masefield, who spent his boyhood here where

> *One road leads to London,*
> *One road leads to Wales.*

It was in these surroundings that he learned to be happy, 'to laugh and be merry', and yet from here in the heart of England he dreamed of the sea and ships.

The great thirteenth-century detached tower of the church once had a shingled, timber spire. Today this churchyard is peaceful, but it was here and in the streets of the town that in April 1645 Prince Rupert, after a forced march from Hereford, met the Parliamentarian troops under Colonel Massey and forced them to return towards Gloucester whence they came.

'Liedeberge' as it was known in 1086 has been in existence since Saxon times, but on the hills to the west, across the Leadon, and to the east are the Iron Age forts of Wall Hills and Kilbury, the former covering 36 acres. Perhaps this great fort was the original Ledbury.

South of the town, along the valley of the Leadon near Donnington is the Vineyard, a south-facing site, formerly terraced. In 1289 the bishop's vineyard south of Wall Hills yielded seven pipes of good white wine. Perhaps this is the site, or it may be that another vineyard has yet to be traced nearer Wall Hills. At least 35 medieval vineyards have been located in the county and recently a few people have started growing grapes and making wine, showing that the climate will still produce a good vintage in most years.

From Ledbury the road towards the Malverns crosses the Silurian ridge and for a while the broken scenery of the Wigmore and Woolhope districts prevails again before meeting the Cambrian rocks and the still older Malvernian range east of Eastnor. Geologically this is a very confused area, for, in addition to the various types of very old rocks, igneous dykes of molten rock from deep beneath the earth's crust were intruded into the Cambrian during the great upheavals of the late Ordovician period. Here is a geologist's paradise and perhaps in some ways, nightmare. Most of this old stone is hard and fit only for rubble for it will not split easily like some sandstones nor cut into ashlar blocks like the later limestones and the Downtonian sandstone. Thus the area is one of timber-framed or uncoursed rubble houses.

Whether the traveller leaves Ledbury by the steep, narrow, road running east from the Homend or by the main Worcester road the route lies through wooded hills and good farmland before reaching the rougher land of the Malverns. The Tewkesbury road soon leaves the main road and leads to the extreme south-eastern corner of the county.

Eastnor is the centre of this area. The estate houses with their thatched roofs and neat timber-framing make a very pleasant picture before one passes through the gateway to the castle along a drive with, on each side, a fine collection of trees from many parts of the

world. The castle was the first of the county's nineteenth-century
medieval revival houses; it was built by Sir Robert Smirke in 1812
using Norman architecture as a model, not gothic. It is a great,
symmetrical building looking down over the lake and the park. The
drawing room decoration and furniture designed by Pugin and the
library by G. E. Fox are two of the most memorable features of the
interior. The park runs away up the hill above the road and is one
of the three remaining deer parks in the county. Unlike Moccas and
Kentchurch the animals here are not the fallow but the red deer and
a fine sight they make against the hillside.

Only a mile or so from Eastnor in a sheltered, secluded valley are
the scanty remains of Bronsil Castle, the fifteenth-century moated
manor house of the Beauchamp family. All that survives is the moat
and part of one of the octagonal towers of the gatehouse, a rather
forlorn, pathetic sight when one thinks of how it must have looked
500 years ago. It is approached through strawberry orchards for here
in this sheltered spot soft fruit grows well.

The road eastwards crosses the county boundary and the Malverns
at a pass through the hills at Hollybush. This is one of the places
where the motorist ought to leave his car and walk if he is really
going to enjoy the scenery and the countryside in this beautiful part
of England. A footpath leads up past the Hollybush quarry to the
Iron Age fortress on Midsummer Hill, recently excavated revealing
a densely populated area with square and rectangular buildings as at
Croft Ambrey and Credenhill. Some of these seem to have used a
timber sill or sleeper-beam, perhaps a forerunner of the medieval
timber-framed houses. The inturned entrances of this 39-acre fort at
one time had timber guardrooms. From Midsummer Hill the Red
Earl's Ditch runs south along the ridge and to the north is Shire
Ditch, a low bank with a ditch on the east side, which follows the
ridge to Herefordshire Beacon and then on to Worcestershire
Beacon. This ditch has been the historic boundary between the two
counties.

Midsummer Hill is 937 feet above sea-level and Herefordshire
Beacon 1,114. The path along the ridge gives magnificent views back

over Herefordshire to the Black Mountains and the the east across the vale of Severn to the Cotswolds. Immediately below to the west is News Wood, to the east down the steeper slope is the fertile farmland of the valley and the winding lanes of the M5/50 with the Severn and Avon on either side.

The Iron Age fort at Herefordshire Beacon guards the pass at Wynds Point just as Midsummer Hill does that at Hollybush. For the energetic the path goes on along the ridge to Worcestershire Beacon across the next pass at Upper Wyche.

From the latter and from Wynds Point roads lead down to Colwall. The church and early settlement are on the hill above the valley of the Cradley Brook, while Colwall Green and Colwall Stone have grown at the other points of a roughly equilateral triangle with sides of about a mile. The last named, so called because of a rock said to have been thrown by a giant, is now the major settlement close to the station.

The old village with the church at its centre has its alehouse at the edge of the churchyard and, across the road, Park Farm is on the site of the manor house of the bishops for Colwall was another of his properties. The church has a fine fourteenth-century roof of arch-braced collar construction with two tiers of curved wind-braces, the lower being cusped to form sexfoiled arches. On the wall of the north aisle is a thirteenth-century encaustic tile showing a man digging, probably one of a series of 12 showing the labours of the months, this one representing March. The capitals of the south arcade should be examined in some detail and in the south aisle is a good brass to Elizabeth Hereford, 1590, which shows her husband clad in armour and their ten children.

Some distance to the west of the village is Hope End, built *c.* 1810 by Edward Moulton who had taken the name Barrett on inheriting a fortune and moved here from Durham when his daughter Elizabeth was an infant. It was a remarkable house in the Islamic revival style which is to be seen in Brighton Pavilion, but unfortunately it was burnt down in 1910, only the stables with their unusual ogee arches remaining to show something of the style of the house. The story of Elizabeth's happy childhood, her riding accident at 15, her mother's death five years later and the move to London where for 20 years she lived in Wimpole Street is well known. After these years of misery she married Robert Browning and spent the last 15 years of her life with him in Florence, bearing him a son but never forgiven by her father who refused to open the letters she sent him.

Two houses close to Herefordshire Beacon deserve a mention. Wynds Point was the home of the great Swedish soprano, Jenny Lind, who died here in 1887, her last concert having been in Malvern. The other, off the road from Wynds Point to Upper Wyche, is Perrycroft, built in 1894. One of the earliest houses by C. F. A. Voysey, it is unpretentious and uncluttered, a complete break with Victorian architecture and a sign of things things to come.

Lower down the valley is Mathon with its early Norman church with some more of the herringbone masonry found at Munsley. In the church the monument to Jane Walwyn, 1617, shows another lady in a hat which was presumably the height of contemporary fashion as at Ledbury.

Cradley church, old school and vicarage dominate the village from the top of their hill, but the black-and-white houses run down to a little valley and up the next hill, a very attractive grouping. The church has a Norman west tower with some peculiar timber strengthening and incorporates a stone carved with Saxon scroll-work in its north wall.

The old school, now the parish hall, is a fifteenth-century jettied building with good moulded bressumers and dragon-beams at the western corners to support the projecting upper floor. With the late Georgian rectory, the church and the late sixteenth-century lychgate it forms a group to be remembered.

This big parish with its variety of timber-framed houses including the unusual herringbone of Upper Vinesend and its narrow, hilly lanes makes a fitting end to travels in this south-eastern corner of the county set between two masses of ancient rock. Here on the Malvernian rocks, probably the oldest pre-Cambrian formation along the

Marches and indeed, east of Anglesey, these villages are set in a different world from the wide valley farmlands of the Wye and the Teme. They are, however, an essential part of Herefordshire and it was here on the Malverns that William Langland, one of England's first great poets wrote his *Piers Plowman*. This little area inspired him 600 years ago and still delights the minds of the twentieth century.

EIGHT

The Golden Valley and Lower Monnow

Why Golden? Is it because of its wealth, the colour of its fields at harvest, the colour of its soil or some other reason? Either of the first two would be applicable, but certainly not the third. A more likely explanation is that the Celtic *dwr,* meaning water, became *d'or* which was finally transferred as a name to the river. Earlier it was called *Straddele* and in 1055 Earl Harold pitched his camp beyond *Straddel* when he was pushing back a Welsh invasion of Herefordshire.

Whatever the origin of its name this 12 miles of valley, rarely a mile wide, with steep hills on both sides, is a fascinating and beautiful part of the county. The river rises in the hills above Dorstone. Here, high up on Dorstone Hill is King Arthur's Stone. This Dark Ages Celtic leader is credited with an Ice Age cave on the Doward and here with a great, late Stone Age burial chamber similar to those found in parts of Wales and Cornwall.

Four hundred feet below down a hill with a gradient of one in four is the village of Dorstone itself with its castle motte at one end and the church at the other on lower ground by the river. Between the two is the typical triangular market-place of the Marcher boroughs and indeed this quiet little village aspired to borough status at one time. It has a market cross with a sundial, not a market-hall. It seems to have been a manor under Clifford, the local family being Fitzponz, and has had its moments of excitement, for Glyndwr severely damaged it in 1404, but more than that, here came one of those who murdered Archbishop Thomas Becket in 1171.

Richard de Brito founded a chapel in the church, probably after returning from completing his 15 years penance in Palestine. In 1889 when the church was restored a stone was found which tells us that John de Brito founded this chapel in honour of the Blessed Mary in 1256. He is said to have been Richard's nephew. The stone can still be seen in the church with a coffin chalice and paten also found in the tomb. Some silver thread and the traces of a long sword found at the same time turned into dust on exposure to the atmosphere.

At the south side of the market-place is the old school founded in 1643. The master was to be a graduate of Oxford or Cambridge with a salary of £20 per annum. Dorstone children received a free education in writing, grammar, rhetoric, oratory and poetry, but those from Peterchurch, Michaelchurch Escley and Craswall were to pay 2s 6d admission and 1s a quarter.

Dorstone was also for a time the terminus of the Golden Valley railway which was opened from Pontrilas in 1881 and extended to Hay eight years later. The $18\frac{3}{4}$ miles of railway cost £300,000, the company hardly ever made a profit and in its whole history owned only one locomotive, two coaches and a brake van. All other rolling stock was rented. The passenger service ceased in 1941 and the line closed in 1957 leaving a rather forlorn-looking platform in a field by the side of the main road.

Before leaving the village centre to visit the church and the railway platform a short walk down Mill Lane is rewarded by the sight of a house, the upper storey of which is constructed of large sandstone slabs on edge, pinned to a timber-framing beneath by big iron pins. It is a form of construction often found in this part of Herefordshire where there are good sandstone flags as part of the local geological formation.

This is a land of castles for only a mile down the valley is Snodhill Castle and two miles beyond that is Urishay. The former belonged to the Chandos family and with its earthwork covers some ten acres. Even in its present ruinous state the twelfth-century keep with its added gate-towers is an impressive sight. Below it is the seventeenth-century stone house of Snodhill Court which no doubt replaced the castle in more peaceful times. Urishay is a motte and bailey, but in this case a seventeenth- and eighteenth-century house was built on the motte and is now ruinous. Also falling into ruins is the now disused chapel, possibly Norman in its origin. This ought to be a scene of desolation, but somehow, surrounded by its great trees, it is not; it seems to be just another peaceful, interesting facet of the Herefordshire scene.

Peterchurch is the hub of the Golden valley. Though never aspiring to borough status like Dorstone it has the finest parish church in the valley, the magistrates' court is held here and the small comprehensive school serving the area is housed in a Victorian mansion in the village. There are two gems in Peterchurch, the church and Wellbrook Manor.

The former is a large and very well-preserved Norman building memorable for its sequence of three arches decreasing in height. These divide nave from chancel, split the chancel into two parts and then divide it from the apse. As the second section is square and slightly bigger than the eastern part of the chancel perhaps it carried a tower as at Much Marcle. The present tower is a thirteenth-century addition. The tall fourteenth-century spire was taken down 25 years ago and has recently been replaced by a plastic one. On the east jamb of the south doorway of the chancel is a scratched sundial with a little hole in the centre for the insertion of a stick to act as a gnomon. In the church is a wall plaque of a carp with a golden chain around its neck. It is said to represent a fish caught in the nearby St Peter's Well. Peterchurch was one of the last places, perhaps the last, in the county to use dog-tongs to put dogs out of church; the dog remover for the period of his office had 'dog-acre', a field adjoining the church, 'for his use and enjoyment'.

Wellbrook Manor is one of the finest of the base-cruck houses of the second half of the fourteenth century. Most of its magnificent woodwork is still intact and the original octagonal chimney of the solar still survives, a very rare sight.

The main road runs along the valley bottom just above the flood-plain. To the east are Merbach, Woodbury and Blakemere Hills with the Wye valley beyond. In the days before the modern motor car these were an effective barrier between the two valleys, the hill out of Dorstone having a gradient of one in four and Stockley Hill from Peterchurch being almost as steep. It is not until below Vowchurch that a gap in the Hills allows an easier route to the Wye and Hereford. At least, the east side is simple, the west side is a network of narrow lanes with sharp turns and sudden steep hills. It is along these lanes that the traveller reaches Snodhill and Urishay from Dorstone and can wander on over the top to the Escley valley.

Below Peterchurch are more defence works, Iron Age hill-forts at Poston and Lower Park Wood. The former is on a spur immediately to the east of the road between Vowchurch and Peterchurch. Even today in the age of the internal combustion engine it is not difficult to imagine prehistoric man standing at this viewpoint where the valley narrows, guarding the route between the fort and the river.

The churches of Vowchurch and Turnastone stand a bowshot away from each other on either side of the river. Local lore has a story that they were built by two quarrelling sisters, but a more likely explanation is that each was built on the low land in the more populous part of its long narrow parish stretching up the hill, Vowchurch on the east side of the Dore and Turnastone on the west. Both churches are small with a bell turret at the west end rather like those of Radnorshire and Breconshire.

Vowchurch is unusual in that the roof is supported on wooden posts as though its early seventeenth-century builders did not trust the older stone walls to bear its weight. A similar construction is to be found in the church at Stretford and in the Quaker Meeting House at Bromyard.

At the end of the sixteenth century Rowland Vaughan proposed 'to raise a Golden Worlde in the Golden Valley, being the pride of all that countree bordering on Wales'. He describes the valley as 'the Lombardy of Herefordshire, the Garden of the old gallants, is the Paradise of all the parts beyond Severn'. He set out his plans for a Utopia in a book *Most approved and long experienced Water Works,* for his dreams depended on a series of irrigation works from above

Peterchurch down to near Bacton. Some parts of this can still be traced today, including remains of his main channel, 'Trench Royal'. This may have been the first of a number of such irrigation works, remains of which can still be seen in the county at the great Vaughan house of Hergest near Kington, Hampton Court, Kingsland, Risbury and elsewhere.

Rowland Vaughan was a great nephew of Blanche Parry (ap Harry) who was born at Newcourt in Bacton parish in 1508. She became an official lady-in-waiting to the young Princess Elizabeth when the latter was only three years old and remained in her service as Keeper of Her Majesty's Jewels and later Chief Gentlewoman of the Privy Chamber until she died in 1589. Her salary was £33 6s 8d a year with a lady for herself, servants, stabling and an allowance for horsemeat. At the queen's coronation she was allowed 'seven yards of scarlet and fifteen of crimson velvet, with one and a quarter yards of cloth of gold, yellow, with work, and three quarters of a yard of cloth of gold, black, also with work'. She was buried at St Margaret's, Westminster, but her heart was brought back to her birthplace to which she left £500 for building an almshouse and 20 cows for the parishioners who were to pay the vicar two shillings yearly for the use of each cow. Her heart is buried beneath the tomb in Bacton Church carved by a follower of John Gildon of Hereford who made some fine Renaissance memorials in and around Herefordshire at this time. Blanche is shown kneeling before her queen. The inscription begins:

> *I Parryehys doughter Blaenche of Newe Courte borne,*
> *That traenyd was in pryncys courts with gorgious wyghts,*

and finishes:

> *So that my tyme I thus dyd passe awaye*
> *A maede in courte and never no mans wyffe*
> *Sworne of Quene Ellsbeths bedd chamber allwaye*
> *Wythe maeden Quene a maede dyd ende my lyffe.*

One other relic of her time surviving in the church is a beautiful

19. *above* A glimpse of Eardisland and the mill stream; 20. *below* Half-timbering in Weobley

altar frontal of several pieces of white silk embroidered with large stylized sprigs of flowers and foliage and numerous small insects, beasts and animals between them. It is said to be the work of Blanche Parry.

A little of her Newcourt Farm remains incorporated in the present house with behind it on the hill the earth motte and bailey of its castle predecessor.

Opposite Bacton the hills on the eastern side get close to the river and the road is forced across both it and the track of the old railway to Abbey Dore. In fact it also crosses the Roman road, a short stretch of which, with tracks on it made by the wheels of vehicles, can be seen in the disused station yard, now part of a farm, at Abbey Dore.

The great sight in Abbey Dore is the church, actually the chancel and crossing of the Cistercian abbey which was founded here in 1147. What remains dates from the late-twelfth and the thirteenth century, Bishop Thomas Cantilupe having consecrated the completed church *c.* 1280. After the Dissolution the local congregation continued to use the church for worship and in 1633 John, Viscount Scudamore, restored the chancel and transepts for use as a parish church. This was reconsecrated on Palm Sunday 1634. The great Renaissance screen and the carved wooden ceilings date from this restoration, the latter being the work of John Abel and the former almost certainly so. It is interesting to compare it with his very similar work on the town hall at Leominster. The tower was built at the same time at a cost of £90. This is a place in which to linger to study Abel's woodwork, to enjoy the medieval tiles reset in the floor of the sanctuary, and to admire the carving of the great medieval stone bosses collected in the ambulatory and transepts. The 12 feet long stone altar with its original consecration crosses still visible and now resting on the re-used bases of three pillars was rescued from a local farmyard. The great east windows are filled with glass dating from the time of the reconsecration with figures of the apostles, John the Baptist and Moses surrounding the central subject of the Ascension.

In the 1960s an Abbey Dore festival was started here to raise funds to keep the church in repair. It attracted world-famous musicians but unfortunately, although keeping the name, the concerts began to be held elsewhere in the county, made no profit and are now no longer held.

Above Vowchurch on the east is its common, a high-up, no-man's-land fascinating to the walker, and to students of the development of small houses and of land tenure. The latter will tell you they are not strictly no-man's-lands, but this does not detract from their interest, nor from the beauty of the views from them. Vowchurch Common has to some extent been tamed; its houses are small and of stone with vast chimneys. A few years ago many were beginning to become ruinous, but their potential as week-end cottages and places of retirement was recognized and many of them have been restored.

Strictly speaking one should now follow the Dulas Brook which joins the Dore at Pontrilas, but that stream is within the land of Ewyas, the subject of a later chapter. Thus the traveller turns to the valley of the Worm which flows into the main river from the east. At its head, down below the Hereford-Monmouth road is Much Dewchurch, a place to be visited in spring when the flowers are out in the hedgerows. The tombs in the church point to two great families having lived in the parish, the Pyes and the Symons. Two of the former, John and Walter Pye, 1547, lie on an altar tomb, the older man with his beard held in his finger while a big Renaissance alabaster and black marble wall monument of 1625 shows the Attorney General Walter Pye, his wife, Joan, and 13 children. Both families lived at Mynde, the Pyes in the fifteenth, sixteenth and seventeenth centuries, the Symons in the eighteenth and nineteenth. Their great house, the Mynde, is on a spur some way south-west of the village, looking slightly forlorn and somehow not fitting into today's landscape.

Two miles along the lanes is one of the county's gems, Kilpeck, the village a mixture of stone houses and black-and-white timber-framing with its Norman church tucked down below the ruined castle on the motte to the west. It is the church which really matters. Superlatives have been used in profusion to describe this church and its carving. Credit must go to the mason who chose the particular red sandstone of which it is built, for after over 800 years the carving is as crisp and clean as when it was first cut. This would not be the case with most red sandstone, but this man knew exactly which stone to use and how to lay it. Much has been written about the Herefordshire School of carving and its origins; some of it has been traced to the pilgrimage of Mortimer's steward, Oliver de Merlimond, to Santiago de Compostela, the beaked figures to Reading Abbey reaching Herefordshire via its cell at Leominster and the dragons to the Scandinavians, and others have looked to Ferrara. Perhaps all these places have had some influence, but there must have been some local, spontaneous feeling behind it as well. Here, at Rowlstone, Shobdon, Wigmore Abbey, Brinsop, Castle Frome, Eardisley and at places even as far away as Llanbadarn Fawr in Radnorshire, these carvers show their influence. There must have been some Celtic, Marcher exuberance in these men which shows itself in the wood carving on the screens and lintels of three and four hundred years later. Some credit must go to local craftsmanship and inspiration and not all to outside influences.

The visitor arriving at the church will probably first notice the south doorway with a vine spray in the tympanum, birds, dragons, beaked heads and a flying angel around the arch. On the jambs are two soldiers in tightly-fitting clothes, one holding a javelin, the other a sword, fat, long dragons with one swallowing another's tail, and acanthus-type interlaced foliage. The corbel table around the church still has 80 of its carved corbels, a dog and a rabbit, a deer, a falcon, two wrestlers, a sheila-na-gig (a female fertility figure) and an Agnus Dei among them. The interior of this small church is just as remarkable, with its chancel arch carved almost as much as the south door but clearly by a different hand, the plain arch into the apse with its carved ribs and windows and its massive font. There was probably a Saxon church here for a corner of the nave has long-and-short work, but it seems to have been rebuilt in the second quarter of the twelfth century. There are so many similarities that the master of Shobdon must have had a hand in some of this as well.

Kilpeck is lovely at any time of the year. The writer first saw it on a dull November day and it was lovely then, but for a surfeit of beauty go in spring when the daffodils are out around the church and the castle and in the lanes leading up to them. Standing on the castle mound it is possible to see in the area encompassed by the roads below the church the boundaries of the village planned with the church and castle.

Here one is back in Archenfield again and the church is dedicated to St David as well as St Mary who seems to have been transferred from the castle. Less than a mile away is St Devereux (or Dubricius) on the way back to the main road.

Farther up this tributary valley are Allensmore and Thruxton. The former has some fine timber-framed houses and a mainly fourteenth-century church with an early stained-glass crucifix in the east window and an unusual fourteenth-century inlaid floor slab in the chancel to Sir Andrew Herl and Joan his wife. Across the main road is Thruxton where close to the church is a mound marked on the OS map as a castle, but from the reputed finds of a nineteenth-century excavation it would seem that it is possibly a Bronze Age barrow.

On the east of the road towards Pontrilas from Kilpeck is Wormbridge Court, a brick house of the hall and two cross-wings shape, but one wing is given over entirely to farming purposes as at Dewsall.

From here to Pontrilas at intervals it is possible to trace the tramway built to carry Welsh coal to Hereford. For a long time it finished at Monmouth Cap just south-west of Pontrilas, but in 1829 it was completed to Hereford. A good stretch of it can be seen between the trees near Howton. Pontrilas is now by-passed and it is possible to stand and admire the fine seventeenth-century stone Court with its timber-framed dovecote. Today the main industry is the saw-mill, but south of the village towards Kentchurch was another of Herefordshire's iron forges, now a hardly recognizable mound in a field between the road and the river, but at one time of considerable importance.

The Dore now joins the Monnow flowing down from Ewyas Lacy and strictly speaking this is the end of the Golden valley. However, it is worthwhile to follow the minor road which runs above the eastern bank of the Monnow as far as the Skenfrith road. It is a beautiful run, the road keeping to the slightly higher ground giving glimpses of the river with the park of Kentchurch on the east and then Garway Hill rising to over 1,200 feet. In places the valley gets very narrow indeed, the hills on both sides coming right down to the river.

Kentchurch Park is one of the three remaining deer parks in the county out of the 35 that there used to be. The Victorian church opposite the park gates replaces an earlier building, but in it is preserved the reclining alabaster effigy of John Scudamore, 1616, erected by his wife Amy who lies in her widow's veil with kneeling figures of their eight sons and a daughter at the sides and an infant in a cradle. The park itself is sheltered by steeply-rising woodland to the north and east, a factor which led to the flooding of the Court to a depth of about four feet after a sudden storm in 1959. The Court was a late fourteenth-century moated manor with a strong defensive tower at one corner. This and other parts of the earlier building and its seventeenth-century additions were incorporated in John Nash's rebuilding in the early nineteenth century. The Scudamores have been here from at least the fourteenth century, probably the longest continuous occupation by any Herefordshire family.

A secluded romantic spot like this seems certain to have its legend and it has—Jack O'Kent, not entirely legend, but partly. In the Court is preserved a portrait of him dressed in a white habit with the old building as a background. He was probably a Lollard priest and may be the John Kent who was vicar of Kentchurch in the late fourteenth century. Legend tells of his dealings with the devil, whom he seemed able to outwit, though he is reputed to have kept a fast horse always ready at Kentchurch in case he needed to make a quick getaway.

Herefordshire has two of the 14 known sites of round churches in England—St Giles, Hereford, and Garway. The former has disappeared, but the foundations of the latter can still be seen in the churchyard, the curves being continued in the chancel arch inside. This should be inspected. It is probably late Norman, perhaps *c.* 1180, but the innermost order is not like the usual work of that period in England; it is lobed like some found in France and is quite probably influenced by eastern Mediterranean carving brought back by the Knights Templar. The church and lands were given to them *c.* 1170. Their lands in England were confiscated in 1312 and in most cases passed to the Knights Hospitallers who in 1326 built the dovecote which can be seen in the adjoining farmyard. It must have been they who altered the church and constructed the fine chancel roof.

On Garway Common close to the road still remain the stand-pipes of the early twentieth-century water supply, a comparatively early example of civil parochial enterprise in this field.

After Garway the road on the English side of the river continues to Welsh Newton, passing on the way Pembridge Castle, a good example of a small, thirteenth-century castle, the forerunner of the defended manor house of 100 years later. It was badly damaged in the Civil War but was restored in 1914 by Dr Hedley Bartlett, its chapel being dedicated in the Greek Orthodox faith. In spite of the rebuilding of the hall block in the seventeenth century and the twentieth-century restoration, a visit to Pembridge Castle still gives an excellent idea of life in a medieval house surrounded by its deep moat.

Those who walk could follow the river past Llanrothal's isolated church to the Cwm, half a mile from Welsh Newton. The present house was built in 1830, but it replaced an earlier building which became a Jesuit college in 1622 in which several priests resided. In 1678 after the scare of the Titus Oates plot Captain Scudamore of Kentchurch raided the Cwm, sent the books to the cathedral at

Hereford, took prisoner Father David Lewis who was martyred at Usk and Father John Kemble. The latter was taken at Pembridge Castle where he spent most of his time with his relatives when he was not travelling the county ministering to the recusants.

In this valley, as in many parts of the county and country there is a story of a secret tunnel, in this case from the Cwm to the old house at Skenchill. There is no evidence of it and it seems very unlikely that it ever existed, for it would be a major engineering feat even today.

Thus in these two quiet valleys the medieval religious life of Herefordshire has left its buildings and its memories in the relics of St Thomas à Becket's murderer at Dorstone, the ruins at Abbey Dore, the carving at Kilpeck, the legend of Jack of Kent, the Templars' round church at Garway and finally at Pembridge Castle and the Cwm where priests of the old faith risked their lives to minister to followers in Herefordshire and across the river in Monmouthshire.

NINE

The Land of Ewyas

In *Domesday Book* only two places are mentioned in this area, both called Ewyas. One gets the impression that this was a waste land, or perhaps a land which was difficult to administer, more likely both. It remained in the diocese of St David until 1852 and much of it still feels Welsh, the place-names being mainly in that language.

Ewyas Harold on the Dulas Brook was one of the county's five boroughs at the time of the *Domesday Book*. The remains of the great motte and bailey at the end of a spur overlooking the village mark the site of one of the few pre-Conquest Norman castles, rebuilt by William Fitz Osbern before the Domesday survey, having been part of his reward for supplying 60 ships towards the invasion of England. The fact that in 1086 Henry de Ferieres held two burgages in the castle indicates that there was some form of borough organization by that date. In the fourteenth century there were two fairs annually and French, Welsh and English merchants came to Ewyas Harold. Today it is an interesting village, very much alive as a community, but lacking some of the beauty of siting that so many Herefordshire settlements have. All traces of the priory have disappeared, not even its site being certain. In the chancel of the church is a cusped early fourteenth-century tomb recess containing a contemporary effigy in high relief of a woman in draped headdress and wimple holding her heart in her hands. No doubt she was a great lady of the castle, but what is the story behind the effigy? In recent years the village has spread itself down the valley towards the confluence of the Dulas Brook and the Dore at Pontrilas.

Ewyas Harold has another such common as Vowchurch. Perhaps because it is farther down river, perhaps feeling rather more of the influence of the lowland culture, some of the houses are of late, thin, timber-framing. It is worth a walk through the bracken to get the view from the top down the Monnow valley.

From here the walker can go down the western side past Great Walk Mill Farm back into the valley of the Dulas Brook. It is a delightful, almost secret valley from Ewyas Harold up to the Trout Inn, passing Dulas on the way. Walk Mill signifies the wool trade once again, for here the cloth would have been fulled. The house and farm buildings are timber-framed and again in some of these sandstone slabs are used in place of wattle and daub. Dulas Church is Victorian and small, standing on its own by the road, but do not just pass by for inside, moved from the earlier church, is a set of 14 carved seventeenth-century chairs. One is dated 1640 and all probably date from about that time. The old church was below the Court, one Norman arch and the level site still remaining in front of the house. This is now a home for retired musicians, a development which had its origins in the Abbey Dore festival. To this seventeenth-century house, almost lost in the enlargement of 100 years later and still more so in the massive Victorian and twentieth-century additions, in its beautiful setting amidst trees down by the Dulas Brook, come famous musicians to meet their old friends and some to stay to end their days in this lovely spot.

Up the valley beyond the Trout the road branches to the right to the commons of Lower, Middle and Upper Maescoed, a vast complex of partially enclosed land with the usual small houses, all within the lordship of Bergavenny (Abergavenny). Here one day the writer and his wife helped to direct some wayward cattle back on to their proper path. The elderly gentleman with them stopped to talk. What was happening to the cows was forgotten in the conversation which followed. He told how for many years up to 1952 he had farmed Great Turnant, which will be mentioned again later, and

how in the bitter winter of 1947 he had buried 210 sheep and a cow
in calf.

The road goes on to Newton and it is in this area that some of
the best of the sandstone quarries are found. They used to produce
very good roofing stone and also the big flat slabs which could be
used for pinning to timber-framing. Behind the main farm in the
hamlet is a well-preserved malt-kiln, looking from the outside almost
like any other farm building. In this high damp area the grain
needed drying out and almost every farm has its malt-kiln
somewhere on the premises, sometimes in the kitchen.

A short mile across the valley is St Margaret's. The church is
typically Welsh, small, with no aisles and no transepts and a stone
and weather-boarded bell turret over the west end of the nave. What
makes the church one of the most interesting in the county is the
magnificent rood-screen, 'one of the wonders of Herefordshire'. It is
in the same class as Llananno in Radnorshire, and Llanfilo and
Partrishow in Breconshire. It has a beautifully carved panelled loft
with coving and is supported on two posts. The upper and lower
rails of the loft are carved with running vine ornament, the coving
is divided into panels with bosses at the intersection of the ribs.
These bosses are all carved, among them being human faces, a lion,
a shield and foliage, while each post is covered with delicate ornament and towards the top each has been cut back to form a niche
with a crocketted and pinnacled canopy. A number of eighteenth-
century texts painted on the walls have been recently restored and
are of considerable interest. This church is one of those rare,
unsuspected gems which are tucked away in the remotest of places
along the Marches.

From St Margaret's and Newton the best route is probably
through Upper Maescoed to Michaelchurch Escley and then up the
road past the school and isolated stone farmhouses to the top of
Vagar Hill and the watershed. Until recently this road was not
properly surfaced all the way over to Cusop; now it is. The views are
magnificent. Michaelchurch Court unfortunately cannot be seen
from the road. It is a stone house with massively thick walls,

probably dating from the late fourteenth century, but today's appearance is that of 1602 when a timber-framed porch was added with fine plasterwork in it.

Down the road towards Longtown is the church with a wagon roof and, much more important, a wall painting of *c.* 1500 of Christ blessing the trades. This and the roof together give an unusually Cornish feel to the church, for this rare subject occurs several times in that county. From the village a road follows the Michaelchurch Brook to Longtown, but for two reasons it is better to leave it rather over two miles below the village and follow a road across the stream towards Lower Maescoed.

The first reason is Old Court, a fine, stone house of *c.* 1400, one of the typical, bigger farmhouses of the lesser gentry of the area. It is of cruck construction and still has the original two-light hall window and some very good post and panel screens. Adjoining it at right angles is a house built some 200 years later, now used as a cartshed. This practice of two houses of near equal status adjoining each other in one yard, frequently with direct communication at the corner from one to the other, is often found in this area and neighbouring Breconshire. It is also found in Cornwall, Lancashire, Suffolk and probably elsewhere. In this area this 'unit' house is possibly a relic of gavelkind, the system of inheritance by which land is shared equally among sons, and which continued quite late in some parts of Wales.

The second reason for taking this road is a magnificent view over Longtown and the Monnow valley from the top of the hill above the village which lies some 400 feet below. At any time this is impressive, looking at Red Daren and Black Daren rising to over 2,000 feet across the valley and then to the north-west above Longtown Castle the steep slopes of the Cat's Back dividing the Monnow from the Olchon Brook. The road crosses the Escley Brook and the Monnow just at their confluence and a few hundred yards downstream the enlarged river is joined by the Olchon flowing in from the north-west.

This was an obvious place for an early settlement and there

appears to have been a church at Clodock for over 1,400 years. Legend tells that Clydawg, King of Ewyas *c.* 540 and a grandson of Brychan, the famous saint–king of Brecknock, was murdered while hunting. The oxen drawing the cart with his body on it refused to cross the ford, the yoke broke and Clydawg was buried nearby. That night a pillar of fire rose from the grave and a church was built on the spot and dedicated to the 'martyr' giving the only dedication to this saint, the name later being anglicized to Clodock. The church with its Norman nave and slightly later chancel is a fascinating building still retaining many of its seventeenth-century box-pews, a fine three-decker pulpit and murals, both medieval and eighteenth century. At the east end the altar-rails are around the altar on three sides, a rare surviving example of this arrangement, while at the west end the gallery built *c.* 1715 for the muscians still stands. A lovely story is told about a bad winter in the last century when the snow prevented the delivery of violin strings from Hereford. Not to be done out of their Christmas music the fiddlers improvised by using greased cords. Behind the pulpit is a slab with a 9th century inscription on it in memory of the dear wife of Guinndas, perhaps the earliest post-Roman inscription in the county.

A little way up the valley by the confluence of the Monnow and the Olchon is the old castle mound at Middle Pont Hendre which was captured by the Welsh in 1146 and was succeeded by the bigger castle at Longtown. It is worth walking slowly from Clodock to the new castle and on to Llanveynoe if there is time. The whole way is full of interest and the views are wonderful.

Longtown borough was laid out in the shadow of the castle which was described in 1186 as the 'New Castle'. This is built in one corner of a much bigger, earlier, square enclosure, which it has been suggested is Roman, but no evidence for this has ever been found. It seems possible that this was Harold Godwin's camp 'beyond Straddel' in 1055. The castle has what is perhaps the earliest round keep in England, raised on an artifical mound in a corner of the earlier defences, with its inner and outer baileys and gateway to the south. With the exception of the castle the only buildings within the early enclosure are the school and schoolhouse, while the space across the road is used as a playing field.

Outside the great square enclosure and running down the hill to the south is the borough of Ewyas Lacy which was set up by the de Lacy family who founded Weobley and Ludlow. Certainly it was in existence by 1234. At the top of the market-place between it and the castle is the thirteenth-century church. This is presumably a borough chapel built to save the people having to walk to Clodock to church. Along its south wall is a stone seat looking down over the market-place now partially infilled with seventeenth-century buildings. From Jew's Lane, west of the castle, there are good views over the Olchon valley to the Red and Black Daren and up the valley to the Cat's Back. Here is peace rarely disturbed by man-made sounds, though the landscape with its hedges and evidence of movement up and down the hillside in times of good and bad farming is itself a product of men over hundreds of years.

In the Monnow valley below the village is Llanwonnog another example of the unit-house system, though this time whilst both houses are of stone both are also of cruck construction, one being probably early fifteenth-century and the other 100 years or more later. There was here as late as 1733 a chapel to St Gwenog, but the interesting story about the site is a legend, not unlike that of Crantock in Cornwall, that in the Dark Ages there was an attempt to build a church here, but every night the work collapsed and this was taken as a heaven-sent sign that the site should be moved.

Up the hill beyond the village the road divides and the more important of the two leads up the Monnow valley to Craswall. Some eight years ago the writer was leading a conference based on Hereford which spent a day in this area, and he was asked by the secretary to check a story told some years earlier by an aged member of the Group who about 40 years before had been cycling from Herefordshire over into Breconshire and had been overtaken by nightfall. He looked around for a friendly light and having knocked at a farmhouse door was given shelter for the night. He remembered the incident well for two reasons, one he had had supper and breakfast off a stone table and two he had shared a room, but not a bed, with the daughter of the house. Within a few days of the end of the conference a vetinerary friend had found the house, the stone table, the friendly farmer and his daughter, who after over 40 years remembered the lame cyclist who had been benighted and stayed with them. The subject of this story had been wounded in the Great War. So much for Herefordshire hospitality and memory.

Craswall Church is at the top of a hill after a series of sharp bends in the narrow road. It was once a complete little community centre in itself. The west end of the church was cut off and at one time used as a school, to the north is a levelled area against the wall used as a fives court and beyond that a hollowed-out area is said to have been a cockpit. If the secular matters were on the north, they were balanced by a stone seat on the south side facing the preaching cross. The church itself is like many of the smaller Welsh churches with a western bell turret, but the chancel roof, dating from the fifteenth century, shows the work of the Marcher craftsmen and still has some painted foliage decoration in the eastern bays.

Beyond the church the road climbs on until it reaches 1,450 feet above sea-level. The view from up here is really grand looking ahead through the gap above Cusop, over the Wye valley to the mountains of Radnorshire, to the south to Black Hill and to the north to Cefn Hill. In the valley of the infant Monnow, between the latter hill and the road, 300 feet below the viewpoint, are the scanty and overgrown remains of the priory of St Mary of the Order of Grandmont founded in 1222 by Walter de Lacy. As an alien priory it was suppressed in the reign of Edward IV since when it has gradually fallen into decay. If it is dry enough to approach the spot the outlines of the church, chapter house and cloisters can still be traced. A lead casket discovered here is said to have contained some of the bones of the martyred virgins of St Ursula, massacred by the Huns on the lower Rhine in 453 and buried at Cologne.

From Craswall to get into the Olchon valley to the south-west the traveller has to go back almost to Longtown before a road leads across to Llanveynoe. It is a route not to be taken on a snowy or icy day. From this little hamlet a road leads around the valley, narrow and very steep in places, the first time the writer drove along it during a wet February he thought he passed over a ford; he was a little surprised next time he came that way to find it was a bridge. On the other hand he and his wife spent over six hours in the valley one fine summer Saturday and did not see another car. In fairness it should be added that this was in 1967.

The church and churchyard of Llanveynoe appear to have been built on the site of a Celtic cemetery reminiscent of Ireland, Scotland and Cornwall. Built into the inside of the south wall of the church are two memorial stones probably dating fron the 9th or 10th centuries. One is an irregularly-shaped stone with a rudely-carved crucifix with the feet in profile rather like a child's drawing. On it are some unusual man-cut hollows and it is just possible that this is a pagan stone re-used by Christians. The other contains the inscription XPC, the first two letters reminding one of the Greek Chi Rho monogram or even earlier Christian crosses, IHC, HAEFDUR FECIT CRUCEM, and alpha and omega. Both were found outside the present churchyard, the former *c.* 1860 above a burial, the latter in 1888.

In the external south wall is built in a plain medieval cross while in the churchyard, again faced by a seat along the south wall is a tall monolithic cross with short arms and a groove down the centre. It probably dates from the 10th to twelfth centuries; so here is a little collection of Celtic crosses better than any other in the county.

From Llanveynoe the road runs along the eastern side of the valley. The first stop for those with time and the inclination to walk should be at Little Black Hill for access to the Cat's Back, Herefordshire's version of Striding Edge. It is not a difficult walk and the views from it in every direction are worth the effort, the path following the 2,000 feet contour for quite a distance. If energy and time allow one should walk on to Hay Bluff at 2,220 feet and over into Breconshire.

Back on the valley road it is noticeable how there are a few quite big old farmhouses and a number of much smaller, later, ones. In the seventeenth century there were a lot of cattle kept on a few farms, in the late eighteenth and nineteenth centuries a number of smallholdings were created here with sheep becoming quite important. Today cattle have come back into their own, sheep are still quite important and most of the later houses are either derelict or holiday cottages. The old, big farmhouses have come back into their own. The most important of these is Olchon Court on the west side of the valley, a fine sixteenth- and seventeenth-century house. Sir John Oldcastle, the Lollard, is supposed to have taken refuge here, but it was certainly not in the present house, though it may well have been in a predecessor on the same site. As one comes down the valley on this side down below is Black Daren Farm and still further is the Great Turnant mentioned earlier in this chapter.

This house, Olchon Court and Black Daren along with a number of others were built as long-houses in which people and cattle were under the same roof, with direct access to each other inside the building, frequently using the same front door. As recently as 1973 there were still a few houses in the county using this highland-zone system of farming. Several houses, including Black Daren and Great Turnant, are of cruck construction.

From Great Turnant the mountain road descends steeply to the Olchon Brook, then almost as sharply up the eastern side to rejoin the more important road between Llanveynoe and Longtown. Near the end of this road Robert Newton, star of *Treasure Island,* found peace on his farm after his harassing experiences on Russian convoys during the 1939-45 war.

If the main road is followed down the valley through Longtown and Clodock the extreme south-western point of Herefordshire is reached at Alltyrynys, at the confluence of the Monnow and the Honddu. This beautiful, mellow stone house in its lovely setting by the river below the hill was once the home of the great Cecil family. Now early eighteenth-century in appearance, it is partially 300 years earlier in construction and was the home of the great-uncle of Elizabeth's Lord Burleigh.

A lane behind the house leads up to Walterstone where the church and the motte and bailey of the Norman castle look across the valley to the ramparts of the Iron Age hill-fort.

Farther along the same road is Rowlstone, again with a big mound, probably a former castle, next to the church. The latter is a remarkable building, second only to Kilpeck in its carving. It is dedicated to St Peter and the stonemason used the cock symbol over and over almost as if to emphasize the apostle's denial of his Lord. The tympanum over the south doorway is of Christ in Majesty, a seated figure in a vesica which is held by four angels flying head downwards, giving us probably an exact replica of how the carving at Shobdon must have looked before being moved into the open. On the west side is the face of a pagan green man with foliage sprouting from his mouth. The chancel arch has cocks in the capitals and in pairs in the abaci. Two upside-down figures on the south capital are said to represent St Peter crucified head downwards. In the chancel are two hinged, wrought-iron candle brackets dating from the end of the fifteenth or early in the sixteenth century and quite possibly unique. Each has five prickets for candles and on the upper rail six birds alternating with fleur-de-lys. The birds have been said to be swans and cocks, but could they not be cocks and hens? And may they have perhaps denoted the men's side and the women's side of the church? A precious possession of the church used to be a black-letter Welsh Bible dated 1588; is it still there?

It is possible to reach Llancillo by a footpath from the Rowlstone-Walterstone road, but the motorist has to cross into Monmouthshire at Pandy or Pontrilas and then cross the river by a track to the north about half way between the two. About a mile up an unsurfaced road after passing under a railway bridge Llancillo with its church, court and castle is reached. In a county with a number of isolated settlements it is one of the most difficult to get at, and probably the most difficult of all the parish churches. Having reached it the journey is forgotten in the peace and solitude of this quiet valley once ruled over by the great Scudamore family whose tombs are in the church. Its pride is its Jacobean pulpit, though the thirteenth-century chest and the long, slender bell in the bellcote, probably of the same date and a rare survival, will interest others.

This isolated hamlet, not as high in the hills, not as far from the towns and the main roads as Craswall and Llanveynoe, nevertheless gives again the peace, the quietness, the away-from-it-all atmosphere which is predominant in this south-western corner of Herefordshire. From this one-time Welsh land of Ewyas one takes away memories of hills and deep valleys, tiny hamlets, churches and their neighbouring castles, isolated communities, strange names, but above all, quietness and peace.

TEN

Leominster to Bromyard

Between these two market towns is a ridge road following the high land of the Dittonian Sandstone mass which forms the basis of this north-eastern corner of the county. It is a broken tract of country with a maze of lanes giving unexpected glimpses of little valleys and sometimes distant views over a wide area of Herefordshire, north into Shropshire, east into Worcestershire and west to the more distant hills of Wales. The succession of 'tons' shows settlement by the Saxons, but the great hill-forts of the area are evidence of the Iron Age and of considerable population in pre-Roman days.

Before following the main road it is worth exploring the northern part of this area by following the road north-east to Kimbolton and Middleton on the Hill. To the south-east beyond the railway and the river as the traveller leaves Leominster is Eaton Hill on which are some indeterminate earthworks known as Castle Comfort, apparently a corruption of *Cwmfordt*. What they signify is not known, but there is no proof that they had anything to do with King Merewalh of West Mercia in the 7th century as has sometimes been claimed. Stockton Bury is a fine eighteenth-century farmhouse which is probably on or close to the site of a Dark Ages settlement and which pre-Dissolution was the property of Leominster Priory. One of the best examples of early sixteenth-century linenfold panelling in the county is to be found in the backs of the choir stalls in Kimbolton Church.

Middleton on the Hill is not a village at all, just a church and farm, off the road, the centre of a parish of scattered farms and small hamlets. The church is interesting as being an almost complete twelfth-century Norman building, though the tower is an addition of some hundred years later. Here time has stood still; even the church bells are all medieval and have not been recast. Together the church and the late seventeenth-century brick farmhouse make a charming picture.

North from Middleton the road passes Upton Court on one side and Nun Upton on the other, both off the road and in Little Hereford and Brimfield parishes respectively. The former still shows its timber-framing, herringbone in type and unusual for Herefordshire. It is a lively composition, one of the county's more impressive houses. Nun Upton still shows its close-set timber-framing on the east front, but the remainder is cased in brick with big Dutch gables which appear to have been added and one rusticated brick chimney stack which must be early eighteenth century and reminds one of the work of Vanbrugh. This house and land was the property of the nuns of Limebrook in Wigmore parish and the timber-framed house probably dates from just before the Dissolution. Later it was for a time the property of the Pitt family and much of its enrichment must date from their ownership.

Also off this road is Lower Drayton where until the early 1960s a patch of rushes was grown for use on the kitchen floor. The house is of cruck construction and there is a square brick dovecote. Brimfield itself lives dangerously on either side of the Hereford-Shrewsbury trunk road, but to the west on Brimfield and Wyson Common are the usual tiny cottages along a maze of lanes. Some of the hedges marking the plots when the commons were divided still exist.

These commons are off the sandstone hills in the low land marking the old route of the Teme, and it is the modern valley of this river which is followed to the east where it cuts through the hills to Little Hereford, probably so named because the parish was a 'peculiar' belonging to the canons of Hereford Cathedral and so outside normal ecclesiastical jurisdiction. The aisleless church is almost entirely thirteenth-century work, but apart from three early fourteenth-century tomb recesses, one of them with ball-flower ornament, the interesting and unusual feature is the wide recess over the chancel arch with a moulded shelf. It was probably for a rood and attendant figures with a rood altar below. Around and south-east of the churchyard between the road and the river are a series of earthworks which are probably the site of the house of the Delamere family.

The narrow gap between the two blocks of high land once carried river, road, railway and canal. Only the first two now remain, but the track of the third and the embankment of the fourth still exist as do the lock-keeper's house on the road to Bleathwood and a railway house east of the church. Thus this quiet little hamlet with its scattered farms in the parish has seen busier days and also an early explorer, for here was born Robert Hughes who circumnavigated the globe with Cavendish and accompanied him on his last voyage in 1591-92. He was an Oxford scholar noted for his work on globes and magnetic variations, having written in 1594 *A treatise descriptive of the globes constructed by Emery Molyneux* and *Brevarium totius orbis*. He is buried in Christchurch Cathedral, Oxford. To the north of the road and river is Bleathwood, again an area of late commons enclosure.

From Little Hereford the best way back to Kimbolton is probably to recross the Teme by the main-road bridge built in 1761 and then go east into Worcestershire for a short time rejoining the Tenbury Wells-Leominster road near Redwood at the foot of Raddle Bank, the hill leading back up on to the sandstone hills. A large area in this north-eastern part of the county was the property of Leominster Priory and it is interesting in the *Heralds Visitations of Surrey,* 1623, to note that a mention is made of 'John Myllett of Redwood nigh Lemster', grandfather of the gentleman making the return. No other Milletts have been found in the area at that time and it seems probable he was the priory steward living at Redwood, though not in the present house which appears to be some 200 years later.

To the south of the main road lies, remote and peaceful, Laysters, again a church and a farm, this time with a castle mound alongside them, the centre of a scattered parish. Apart from its poetic setting under a big cedar tree the church is worth a visit for its fine late fourteenth-century roof with foiled wind-braces forming quatrefoils. Again, fine early houses remain and a drive along these leafy lanes is rewarding for the peace away from main roads and for the glimpses of these houses especially Cinders, Wilden and Woonton Court. It is surprising to suddenly come across a herd of Guernsey cows after seeing on most farms the big red-and-white Herefords and the black-and-white Friesian dairy cows, but here they are, smaller, brown and white, but giving rich milk and cream.

Farther along the road and back in Kimbolton parish is Moor Abbey, a former possession of Leominster Priory, a post-Dissolution house but with part of an earlier moat and fishponds still surviving. Instead of going back to Leominster it is probably better to take the minor road to the south-east at Stockton Cross and follow it until it meets the Leominster-Pudlestone road.

This is a fascinating, winding road, with constant ups and downs, not the route to follow if one is in a hurry. Away to the north on a spur between two streams is Bach Camp, one of the Iron Age hill fortresses mentioned earlier. It is clear from the houses that good use was made of the local stone though there are timber-framed buildings as well, neither material apparently being predominant. The church at Pudlestone has an interesting and puzzling tower, for at first sight it appears to be pre-Conquest with long-and-short work quoins and a distinct batter in the walls. However, the lancet windows appear not to have been inserted and are apparently early thirteenth-century in date. In spite of its early appearance it would seem that the tower is not earlier than *c.* 1200. The glass in the aisle windows seems to have been designed by Pugin for the owner of the castellated mansion of Pudlestone Court, now a school, built late in the 1840s.

The road south past the gates to the Court, leads to the Leominster-Hatfield road which runs along the hillside overlooking the Humber Brook and the track of the old railway line from Leominster to Bromyard. Down in this valley below the road junction is Forde Abbey, a fine timber-framed, late medieval house.

The church at Hatfield is one of the few in the county with some herringbone masonry in it, probably from the late eleventh century, with a doorway and tympanum of about the same age. One of the bells is of the rare, early, almost cylindrical shape and must date from before *c.* 1260 when the shape changed. Unfortunately what was probably the earliest brick house in Herefordshire, Hatfield Court Farm, has disappeared. It was built *c.* 1595, almost certainly earlier than both Hellens, *c.* 1615, and Gatley Park, *c.* 1634. There is a little more of a village atmosphere about Hatfield than places like Laysters, but not much; it is again a parish of scattered farms, often half-hidden for much of the year by their orchards and a delightful sight, especially in May when the blossom is out.

Thornbury is another hilly, scattered parish but the important sight in the parish is Wall Hills, an Iron Age hill-fort enclosing about 23 acres. It is on a flat-topped hill about 760 feet above sea-level, the great rampart rising in places 40 feet from the present ditch level. Apart from the fort itself, the view is magnificent. To the west of the road from Hatfield is Park Farm which is surrounded by a bank with an external ditch which was probably the park pale. It encloses about 97 acres and probably separated the cultivated land from the forest or park surrounding it.

This part of the county, as was seen in chapter 4, seems to have more than its share of deserted and demolished churches. At Bredenbury the earlier church was pulled down in 1876 after the building of the Court, now a school, and a new church built farther up the hill. The view across the valley to the north and east as one climbs up to Bredenbury from Bromyard or goes down the hill eastwards from the village is reminiscent of that east of Brockhampton. North-east of Bredenbury along a minor road are the scanty remains of Wacton Church which was pulled down in 1881. The Court and the old castle motte stand by the churchyard; once again there is this grouping at the centre of a parish.

In bad weather, snow or fog this stretch of road through Bredenbury and on to Docklow is dreaded by motorists for it is high and exposed. Across the fields to the south of the road is Grendon Bishop Church, one of the most isolated in the county; it is 300 yards from Grendon Manor, the nearest house to it.

At the top of the hill west of Steens Bridge a Roman road crosses the Leominster-Bromyard road and to the south this leads to Blackwardine and Humber. In 1881 when the railway was being constructed the navvies found quantities of Roman coins, a gold bracelet and ring, lots of pottery fragments, skeletons and some form of hypocaust or kiln. Recent excavations have found a hypocaust and it seems that there must have been a reasonable-sized Roman settlement close to their road, perhaps a villa.

Humber Church stands close to the rectory and Court, once again a small grouping, in this case not even central to the parish, but on the western edge of it. The chancel roof of the church is a very unusual one for this area, with crown-posts and cusped two-way struts, probably dating from the fourteenth century. The porch of the same date is also of interest.

South of the church and Court is Risbury Camp, another great Iron Age hill-fort, covering about 28 acres. High up above the Humber Brook it is in a strong defensive position. Today down in the valley below are Risbury Mill and Risbury Court, eighteenth-century houses making an attractive grouping in this quite deep valley. Risbury is the main settlement of Humber parish, the others being scattered farms as seems to be the rule on this sandstone mass.

The extensive parish of Pencombe is an even better example of this for even before leaving the parish of Humber a signpost to Marston Stannett points north and adds 'No Through Road'. This hamlet is one of the series of scattered, isolated settlements on this high land, rather like Grendon Bishop mentioned earlier. However, there are still two sizeable farms and a church as well as a number of cottages, and there is probably more of the atmosphere of the medieval settlement here than in most of these hamlets. There were 15 people here in the Poll Tax returns of 1377, and it cannot have changed a great deal in the 600 years in between. Lower Marston farmhouse, now cased in stone, is an early cruck building, but its fine timber-framed porch is still there for all to see from the road.

The parish boundary is a stream in a deep valley out of which one climbs to over 800 feet on the way to Pencombe village. On both sides, away off the road, are scattered farms with names which are centuries old, Maidenhyde, Sidnall, and others and, in many cases, houses which have evidence of considerable age. Pencombe itself is in a hollow with a number of old houses around a church rebuilt in 1864-5 in a Norman and Transitional style. Across the farmyard by it is an enormous seventeenth-century dovecote, while across the road below the old forge is a washing pool, an unusual relic of former days, reminiscent of the *dhobi* pools in India.

Grendon Warren, once extra-parochial, is another isolated settlement, along a rough gated road across fields. Here also was a chapel, now used as a farm building. Perhaps the two Grendons and Marston Stannett, all three with churches, show how isolated and difficult of approach they were in earlier times, though on the other hand, they were in the fourteenth century small nucleated settlements with their farms and fields.

Even today in spite of some modern houses Pencombe is not on a classified road and seems strangely away-from-it-all in a different world from the modern rush and bustle. The road from Humber continues eastwards crossing the Leadon, the parish boundary again being marked by a stream, and then up to Crowles Ash where the house on the north of the road was one of a number with a hop-bagging hole just inside the front door, showing that in earlier days the hops were dried in the house. Eventually the main road is rejoined at Flaggoners' Green on the western edge of Bromyard. Until a few years ago a rather fine half-hexagonal brick toll-house stood here, a contrast to the square stone one which still stands at the eastern end of the town.

Bromyard, once a borough sending members to Parliament, lost its urban status in 1968 when it became part of the Rural District and six years later even that authority disappeared becoming part of the Malvern Hills District in the new county of Hereford-Worcester.

In spite of these changes the town still remains a flourishing market centre.

As at Leominster, Ross, Ledbury and Hereford itself there is no sure evidence of settlement in prehistoric or Roman times, even the great hill-fort of Thornbury being three and a half miles away. Like those other towns the church played an important part in its origins and development for in Saxon times it was a minster, the ecclesiastical centre for a considerable area and later, like Ledbury and Ross, was a portionary church, the priests being responsible for the churches in the great manor of Bromyard as well as the mother church in the town. This gave rise to some confusion and claims that it was collegiate, but this was not the case.

The fine church has grown from a late-Norman cruciform building with a central tower, though most of the latter in its present form is fourteenth-century. The late twelfth-century south doorway has been reset in the aisle built some 130 years later and above it are a figure of St Peter and a consecration cross which may well be from the pre-Conquest church. There are a few other reset stones in the walling which could be from the earlier building. Altogether there are eight tomb recesses, all of them fourteenth-century in date. Bromyard appears to have been a favourite residence of the bishops of Hereford judging by the number of ordinations carried out there, and the ceremony connected with these may account for the size of the fine chancel, rebuilt early in the fourteenth century. In the church is kept the Bushel Measure dated 1670, probably removed from the old market-hall at the time of its demolition.

Where the bishop had his manor house or palace is not certain, but it seems possible that it was on the site of the later vicarage, now the District Council offices. Equally there is no sure evidence of the Portioners' houses except that one appears to have been towards the south-east of the churchyard near the old grammar school building.

The latter was founded in 1394 and refounded after the confiscation of the chantries. The little two-roomed building which is now part of the primary school could be from either date, but has been re-roofed and so altered that it is very difficult to be certain.

Like Kington, Bromyard has lost its railway and where the station once stood, down the hill from the old grammar school, there is now a small, industrial estate.

The Market Square once had a timber market-hall apparently very much like the one at Pembridge, but this was demolished in 1844. The more important market days in Bromyard must have led to chaos in the town for cattle were sold in High Street, sheep in Sheep Street (Old Road), pigs in Rowberry Street, general merchandise in Broad Street and the Market Square and horses in Milvern Lane. There was no by-pass in those days. One of the sports for the boys of Bromyard, even into this century, appears to have been to tease the sheep until they jumped the hurdles which penned them in and then help the farmer to get them back.

The early borough lay-out with the narrow burgage plots running back from the street is still very clear on either side of High Street and Broad Street. There has been encroachment here as in Hereford for the old cellar line in Broad Street is one room back from the present street line, later building, no doubt, having taken place on the space once occupied by the *seldae* or stalls. The variety of shop-fronts along these two streets is fascinating, some of them being excellent examples of local nineteenth-century design and craftsmanship.

Just as at Leominster and Kington there are two good assembly rooms. The bigger is behind the fine timber-framed Falcon Hotel and whilst not as elaborate as the Black Lion at Leominster, it is of the same type, whilst that at the Hop Pole is in the same position as the one at the Royal Oak at Leominster, across the front of the building. Again the question must be asked as to which was Whig and which Tory.

There are a number of quite fine timber-framed buildings and some good brick in the town, but Tower House built in 1630, is the outstanding example, its close-set framing, porch and decorated gable showing up well from the by-pass. The gateway to its yard is of moulded stonework and may well have been brought from the church or one of the places connected with it.

One of the most interesting buildings in the town is not easily seen and is in a bad state of repair. This is the brick Quaker Meeting House, with timber posts and hammerbeams supporting the roof; it dates from the first few years of the eighteenth century. In Sherford Street is a fine early eighteenth-century Congregational Chapel and below it the old Police Station and Gaol dating from *c.* 1840.

Although Bromyard is so close to the little river Frome it is above it and aloof from it and one suspects that the river never really played much part in the life of the town. Having crossed it at Petty Bridge one has left Bromyard and at once is out on the Downs emphasizing the scattered nature of the settlements served by the town.

In this chapter the traveller has visited some of the lesser-known parts of the county, a strange, almost secretive area, yet a delightful one with a fascinating background. It is a district of good farms and farmland; Bromyard and Leominster are all the richer for serving it.

ELEVEN

The Land of the Mortimers

For almost a thousand years the administrative centre of this extreme northern part of the county was Wigmore. Stripped in 1930 of its position as headquarters of the Rural District, losing its magistrates court in 1971, its vicar in 1971, it still has its ruined castle and abbey and is the educational centre for the area. Yet here for 400 years came kings and queens, bishops and princes and the greatest in the land.

The Romans had a fort here, east of the present Bury Farm, though nothing can be seen on the ground today. We read in the *Anglo-Saxon Chronicle* that in 921 King Edward had a fortress built at *Wigingamere* which was unsuccessfully attacked by the Danes in the same year. Whether or not this was Wigmore is not known. Legend has it that Edric the Wild, the local Hereward the Wake, was Lord of Wigmore, but this is not borne out by *Domesday Book*, 1086, by which time Wigmore was a borough with a castle.

The castle of those days was probably the small motte and bailey just west of the church, and closely related to the streets of the borough lay-out, not the great mound and ruins which can be seen today farther west. The earliest part of this later fortress appears to be the twelfth-century shell-keep on top of its great mound. Much of the curtain and its wall-towers and gateway is fourteenth-century work. There is no public access to the castle, but the owner is normally generous in giving permission to visit it. To this centre of Mortimer power among others came Llewellyn, Prince of Wales,

Queen Isabella, Edward I, Edward III, and 'dark-eyed' Gladys, daughter of Llewellyn, who became the wife of Ralph de Mortimer. The King's Council met here and great tournaments were held, perhaps the greatest being in 1330. These may have been the reason for the great enclosure north-east of the castle which ran down across the present main road and can still be traced as a crop-mark today.

The male line of the Mortimers died out early in the fifteenth century, but Edward, Duke of York, a great grandson, became King Edward IV.

Earlier than the present castle is the main part of the parish church with late eleventh-century herringbone masonry and a tufa window; it must have been a big Norman building. Apart from the fine roofs there are two other notable pieces of woodwork in the church—the early sixteenth-century decagonal pulpit with seven linenfold panels and the stalls in the choir with poppy-head ornament and arranged in Puritan fashion to take a central altar. Beneath the present altar is a tombstone to 'that Rev. and learned divine' Dr Alexander Clogie who was vicar of Wigmore from 1647 to 1698, a real 'Vicar of Bray' who not only survived changing regimes and fashions, but became well-known for his sermon *Vox Corvi* of which a few contemporary printed copies still survive.

Wigmore retained its borough status for almost 800 years though it never had representation in Parliament. The timber-framed market-hall, open on the ground floor and with a meeting-room above stood at the head of the market-place or 'pavement' looking down the village street until the middle of the last century. Like so many of these Marcher markets it was triangular in shape, the main street running out at the apex and the hall standing at the base.

Aaron Thomas was a Wigmore man who was on H.M.S. *Boston* during the Napoleonic Wars and wrote the first real account of Newfoundland. He was born at the Bury Farm in 1762 and his brother founded a silversmith's business in New Bond Street, London which was in existence until bombed in 1941.

Across the valley is the ruined abbey founded in 1179 by Hugh de Mortimer. It was first at Shobdon, *c.* 1140, then for a short time at Aymestrey and then in Wigmore before finally settling at Paytoe. Its site in the village may well have been at the top of Jacob's Ladder, for the monks complained about the steep descent to fetch water and about the language of the locals. Today little remains of the 1179 complex except the gatehouse and the abbot's lodging, now a private house.

Mention has already been made of the gypsies. In 1970 a gypsy funeral was held in Wigmore and it will not be forgotten for a long time for two reasons, the floral decorations and the fight and for that matter a packed church. The grave was a mass of flowers arranged symbolically, the gates of heaven ajar, the chair with the broken leg signifying one member missing from around the table and the horse all beautifully made. The fight would have been recognized by Hazlitt, bare fists, crowd and timekeeper; unfortunately (or perhaps fortunately) it blocked the main road at the 'pavement' and had to be stopped to let the traffic pass.

From Wigmore, best of all from the castle, there is a view north over the basin formed during the Ice Age when the old southern route of the Teme through Aymestrey was blocked by the terminal moraine from a branch of the Wye valley glacier. As the ice melted a lake formed and the shore-line of this can still be seen in the lane southwards from Leinthall Starkes. Eventually the Teme made its way out at the lowest point and cut the present gorge running north past Downton between steep Silurian limestone cliffs just as the Lugg did at Kinsham.

From here can also be seen part of one of England's first fully documented enclosures, for in 1772 Wigmore Moor and three areas of woodland in the parish were enclosed by the burgesses of the borough. The straight-hedged plots on the moor looking like medieval strips have deceived some historians into thinking that that is what they were, but this land was open, common grazing until the late eighteenth century.

From Wigmore Abbey, and perhaps before that from a collegiate foundation in the present parish church, priests served the little

Norman churches around the edge of the basin. These are Leinthall
Starkes, Elton, Aston, Burrington and Downton, all originally rather
similar, small churches. The first three are along the southern
and eastern edges of the old lake along the one-time turnpike
road to Ludlow. Leinthall Starkes will be remembered for the
glimpse of a fine pair of crucks just opposite the little green and its
church down across fields well away from the village. Near it are
a series of mounds; so perhaps the original settlement was here
and moved up to higher ground. The church has a simple rood-
screen, but the interesting feature is the evidence at the west end
of an annexe, a type of narthex, not normally found in a small
church.

Elton also has a simple rood-screen, but perhaps the most important feature is the fine coat-of-arms of Elizabeth I. The brick Hall,
next to the church, is a pretty Georgian building, but its wing seems
to be the cruck building described in a document of 1400. However,
Elton is famous for Thomas Andrew Knight's experiments in fruit
raising. Here were developed new and better strains of cherries and
plums and here came Sir Humphry Davy. Frances Knight tells us
how concerned she was about the famous scientist coming to visit
her father, but later all was well, Davy was younger than she had
expected, he was dark and handsome and he came and played on the
lawn.

Literally just around the corner is Aston, another tiny settlement
with a great motte rising above its moat east of the church. The
latter is an almost complete example of Norman building with a
beautifully preserved tympanum of the Agnus Dei over the north
doorway and some very early, red ashlar painting with flowers on
stalks on the nave walls.

From this delightful little building it is probably worthwhile
returning through Elton to turn left up the aptly named Killhorse
Lane just south of the hamlet. The steep, narrow road climbs up
through Mortimer Forest and at the top follows an old meltwater
channel down the Goggin. Along it are some typical small
commons cottages. As it bears around to the left towards Richard's

Castle a view opens out over the Teme valley as it goes east towards Tenbury.

In Richard's Castle the traveller should turn left at the first crossroads up the hill towards the old borough and church. Here is one of the earliest Norman castles in England, having been founded *c.* 1050 by Richard le Scrob, one of the nobles whom Edward the Confessor brought over from France. The borough status also may be pre-Conquest, but certainly it was a borough by 1086. The little remaining stonework is all post-Conquest, but the motte and bailey seem to be the original work of *c.* 1050. There is some evidence of an enclosure around the borough and the triangular space east of the churchyard is probably the original market-place.

The old church is now rarely used, but is interesting with a detached south-east tower. As befitting its status as the church of a borough there was a fine Norman building here. Most of the other work is fourteenth-century and the typical ball-flower ornament appears in the aisle east window. The stained glass in the south aisle is quite interesting as are also the seventeenth-century box-pews; because the church has been little used for a long period it gives a good impression of what many must have been like before their nineteenth-century restorations.

All the way along the road down to the village are a number of timber-framed houses, some of them very interesting and including a good dovecote at Court Farm. Once back on the main road it is easy to see why Richard's Castle has tended to move down the hill.

The road is known as the Portway and was the old main road from Ludlow to Leominster, but today the trunk route is further east. Between the two is Orleton, an attractive village of timber-framed houses with the manor house at one end and the church at the other. The former has a close-set timber-framed front and appears to have been re-windowed *c.* 1620 when the semi-octagonal oriel was added. Alexander Pope, the poet, stayed here when he was perhaps hoping for the hand of Miss Blount, daughter of the owner of the house.

The church is basically Norman and the best piece of this period is the font, the work again of the Herefordshire School of carvers. It shows nine standing figures, probably apostles, each under an arch. The pulpit is a fine mid-seventeenth century piece of work.

Two men of importance in their time have come from this little village. One was Adam of Orleton, bishop in turn of Hereford, Worcester and Winchester, who was partially instrumental in the deposition, and perhaps death, of Edward II. The other was Arthur Keysall Yapp who introduced the Red Triangle symbol for the YMCA during the 1914-18 war and was responsible for raising over £3 million.

Orleton fair is on St George's Day, 23 April, and people listen for the cuckoo at this time, for it used to be said he came to it to buy a horse.

The western part of the parish rises to join the long line of woodland running from Bringewood on the Shropshire border to Bircher Common, a beautiful, peaceful area to wander in, where one's only companions are the deer and the smaller mammals, the birds and the hum of insects.

South of Orleton on the Portway is Luston another attractive village of timber-framed houses, this time along the main road. East of it between the two roads again is Eye with more timber-framed houses and two bridges, one over the railway, the other over the old Leominster-Mamble canal. North of here is the Putnal tunnel, still with its arch at each end and although the passage is still intact here in fact a fall has blocked the way through.

Eye Manor is well-known for nine enriched plaster ceilings, dating from 1680 when the house was built for Ferdinando Gorges, a Barbados sugar and slave trader. From the plain brick outside one gets no idea of the richness of plasterwork, panelling and stairway that are inside. Also noteworthy in the house are the examples of the art of corn-dolly making and the beautiful bindings and printing of books produced by the Golden Cockerel Press.

In the church adjoining the manor are two altar tombs to the Cornewall family with alabaster effigies.

Across the fields and down a drive is Berrington Hall built for

Thomas Harley by Henry Holland in 1778-81. Capability Brown-worked on the grounds ahead of his father-in-law. It is a simple house and its pinkish sandstone, quarried a few hundred yards away, fits into the Herefordshire landscape well. Inside, every room on the ground floor is exquisitely decorated, while in the centre of the house is the splendid staircase, all today beautifully maintained by the National Trust.

From Luston a road leads to Yarpole, pleasantly set along a stream away from any main road yet quite a sizeable little place. Across the stream in the centre of the village is a disused medieval gatehouse, often known as the 'bakehouse', which it was for part of its history. There are some attractive timber-framed houses near the church, but the detached bell-tower is of even more interest. It is smaller than that at Pembridge, but of the same type and more complete in that some of the cross-bracing is still intact. In the church itself is a crown-post roof, a rare form of construction in Herefordshire. It is interesting that this church has both an unusual roof and an even more unusual form of detached belfry; what influences were at work in this comparatively isolated village?

Above Yarpole is Bircher, a township in the same parish, again with a number of good black-and-white buildings and a brick dovecote. Higher up is Bircher Common, a considerable open space at the end of a long line of forest. Those who were living around here in 1968-69 will not easily forget the glow in the night sky from cattle being burnt on the common during the severe foot-and-mouth epidemic. It is a sight every countryman fears and one which nobody wants to see again.

From the common there are magnificent views away to the Malverns, to the Black Mountains and to Shropshire. For those prepared to walk this is an excellent way to get to Croft Ambrey, a great Iron Age hill-fort perched on a spur looking down over Leinthall Earles and Wigmore. This site was occupied for about 600 years from 550 B.C. until the Roman conquest and eventually covered about nine acres as well as an annexe of about 12 acres which seems to have been little used. A population of at least 500 lived in tiny rectangular houses along streets while at one stage there were rectangular stone and timber guard-rooms at both entrances. Another smaller Iron Age fort, Pyon Wood, faces Croft Ambrey across the valley to the west and there are others at Brandon just south of Leintwardine and at Coxall Knoll west of Brampton Bryan.

Across the narrow valley to the north is Gatley Park, one of the first brick houses to be built in Herefordshire. It was built in the 1630s by Sir Sampson Eure, a London merchant, and stands warm and mellow on its bluff looking down over Leinthall Earles and away to the hills beyond. The little village in the valley below has a tiny Norman church with a good fifteenth-century roof, an attractive, well-restored, seventeenth-century almshouse and among other timber-framed buildings, the old school, in use until 1962. Behind this is a quarry where the brachiopod *Conchidium knightii* laid down some 400 million years ago is now extracted in its fossilized state for roadstone.

It is interesting to think of the way this rather remote area was well provided for by schools bequeathed by local people long before compulsory education. Aymestrey as early as 1516, Leinthall Earles and Wigmore in the seventeenth century, Leinthall Starkes, Brampton Bryan, Lucton, Little Hereford and Leintwardine in the eighteenth all had schools. It was a remarkable achievement.

A lane leads to Leinthall Starkes and another from there across the Wigmore basin to Burrington, an almost lost hamlet in the hills, but important for its cast-iron tomb slabs, the finest collection outside the Weald. The earliest of the eight dates from 1619. Why are they here? In Burrington parish was Bringewood Hall, the home of the Knight family, the great ironmasters, whose works were in the parish on the banks of the Teme.

Later the family moved to Downton which is down river from Burrington along a road which runs close to the Teme gorge. For those with time and energy the walk up over the hill to the north, across the valley and then along to Bow Bridge is to be recommended. This bridge carried the Ludlow–Leintwardine road across the Teme until the route was diverted to avoid the grounds of

Downton Castle. It is deep in the gorge. Limestone cliffs tower above it where the Teme has cut its route after flowing across the Wigmore basin. It is typical limestone scenery, a truly magnificent sight, yet very little known.

From the bridge the road climbs up to old Downton, Downton on the Rock. The scanty remains of the Norman church and the castle mound are evidence of its importance before the Knight family founded a new village at Downton Castle close to the great house built between 1772 and 1778, though the new church was not erected until 1861. This new mansion, in a dramatic setting above the gorge, was one of the first castellated Romantic buildings in England. Richard Payne Knight put into practice here his theories which he and Price propounded together and which his kinsmen, the Johnnes family, used at Croft and Hafod. Two bridges were built across the river to link the village and house with the ironworks, now completely overgrown and deserted and in any case on private property. Today school, chapel, houses and works are all deserted, yet here were produced cannon for the Civil War and the tombstones at Burrington.

An ironworks of this size required power, provided by the Teme, ironstone from the Clee Hills, limestone from local quarries, and lots of timber for charcoal. This last came from the local woods and forests and as early as the late sixteenth century the forest of Deerfold was being stripped for the Downton forges.

Deerfold is a fascinating area on the hills between Wigmore and Lingen to the west. It was up here that there were anchorites for whom the advice in the *Ancrene Wisse* was written early in the thirteenth century. Perhaps these 'anchorites' were the first nuns at the nunnery at Limebrook which was founded about this time. There are a few remains of it in the deep, beautiful valley of the Lingen Brook still overlooked by the fine cruck house of the nuns' home farm. Indeed, the nuns owned some fine houses and their associated farms some as far away as Stoke Bliss and Clifton-on-Teme in Worcestershire. For over 300 years the little group of six nuns and the attendant community lived here in this peaceful spot until in

1539 they were forced to hand over their possessions to Henry VIII. In a lane close by still grows the asarabacca, a plant used for medicinal purposes in medieval times, and found in only some half-dozen localities in the British Isles.

One of the most impressive of their houses was Chapel Farm on Deerfold, built *c.* 1400 on land given to the nunnery early in its existence, some of the place-names in the early thirteenth-century document still continuing today. This house, a private dwelling off the road, has some very fine woodwork in its hall and parlour.

To the social historian Deerfold is very interesting for here, almost unchanged, survive the hedges, roads and buildings of the enclosure of the 1820s. No doubt this was done at the instigation of the bigger landowners to take advantage of the Corn Laws, grain still being grown today in the bigger fields, but the interesting fact is that the smallest of plots, down to less than half an acre were enclosed. The writer has seen the red squirrel on Deerfold, nor far from the Cross of the Tree where an old oak marks the crossroads on Ongar Street. One cannot help wondering if this straight 'street' across this upland block marks a Roman road westwards from Wigmore.

Off the steep scarp at the western edge of Deerfold is the pleasant village of Lingen, a mixture of stone and timber-framed houses with its big motte and bailey behind the seventeenth-century Court House. The church has been rebuilt, but its pews are of early sixteenth-century date with a heavy roll-moulding and are reputed to have come from the nunnery church at Limebrook.

West of Lingen are more hills and a wonderful maze of narrow lanes leading to isolated farms in the middle of which is a crossroads with a chapel by it. This is Willey. Favoured visitors to the writer get brought up here, preferably in the hour before sunset, to explore this lovely area. For two miles, in places at a height of over 1,250 feet, the road runs along Reeves Hill and Stonewall Hill, along the boundary between England and Wales. Up here there is peace and the hills and the sheep and the cattle are part of an almost unchanging world. At one farm the field immediately next to the present house yields Bronze Age relics; man chose his sites early and has stayed on them.

From the peace and the breeze at the top come back to Willey and then back to Letton via Willey Lodge, timber-framed, overlooking the road, and Birtley. At Letton look at the gateposts of the farm; the strange animals could have come from Kilpeck, but probably came from Wigmore Abbey as did stones used in various buildings in Adforton two miles along the road to the east.

At the confluence of the Teme and Clun Leintwardine was bound to be a place of some importance and here above a ford the Romans built *Bravonium*. Their first fort was at Jay Lane at the top of the village; this was followed by a fort at Buckton and finally at Leintwardine, though there was a civilian settlement at the last place from an earlier date. Outside the walls at the bottom of the village was a bath-house. These Roman sites have been carefully excavated over the past 20 years, but there is little to see on the ground.

Some evidence of the fort can be seen in the church where the chancel is much higher than the nave because the Roman eastern rampart runs beneath it. The beautiful, well-carved series of choir stalls with their misericords are reputed to have come from Wigmore Abbey. On either side of the east window the fragments of the early fifteenth-century stone reredos show what a fine piece of work it must have been before its destruction.

Leintwardine on the Teme and the Clun is a fisherman's village and on the long series of meanders through the terraces of glacial gravel upstream and downstream hopeful figures with rod and line look for likely places to make a catch.

Up river along the Teme past Walford on the south and Buckton on the north, each with its castle mound, is Brampton Bryan. On the way, just south of the main road, is a Bronze Age bowl-barrow over 60 feet long.

Brampton Bryan first presents a delightful picture of timber-framed houses around two sides of a triangular village green. The third side is taken up by the main road into Wales and, at its edge, a fine yew hedge around the garden of the house and castle. There is more timber-framing along the minor roads to the north and south. The former also leads to the church, quite a big, rectangular building of 1656. The earlier church had to be rebuilt then because of the damage caused in the siege 12 years earlier. It is simply a 'preaching box' to suit the religious doctrines of the Commonwealth and of Sir Robert Harley its builder, a staunch Puritan for whom altars, chapels and decoration held no attraction. Its roof is a most unusual double hammerbeam and it has been suggested that parts of it may have come from the castle. In a recess is a late fourteenth-century effigy of a woman, presumably a Harley.

The Harley family have been here since 1309 when Sir Robert de Harley of Harley in Shropshire married Margaret Brampton. It was he who built the great gatehouse of the castle which still remains, and from here came a later Sir Robert, the great Puritan leader; Robert, first Earl of Oxford, Prime Minister to Queen Anne and Edward, second earl, friend of Gay, Pope, Prior and Swift. It was Lady Brillianna, wife of the seventeenth-century Sir Robert, who defended the castle against the Royalists in 1643 for seven weeks. She died in the October and in the following April after a three-week siege Colonel Wright was forced to capitulate. A few weeks later the castle, the library, works of art and manuscripts were all destroyed.

A new brick house was built close to the ruins of the castle in 1663 and this was incorporated into the present Georgian house in 1748.

The Harleys also owned Wigmore Castle for 350 years and it is interesting to note the group of Herefordshire names in London marking the Harley property there; Harley Street, De Vere Street, Mortimer Street, Wigmore Street, Wigmore Hall all take their name from the family and its connections.

Brampton Bryan fair is held on 22 June, and there was an old saying to the effect that the horse bought by the early cuckoo at Orleton was sold here before his departure.

Fittingly this chapter has finished with a castle and a great family just as it started with a castle and an earlier great family, for this is a land of castles and was a land of Marcher warfare. Perhaps it is right that having entered the county in the south-east from England the traveller should leave it in the north-west for Wales.

Thus having followed the Teme back from its gorge at Downton, across the Wigmore basin, through the gravel terraces the traveller reaches the end of his Herefordshire journey as the river comes down from Shropshire and Wales and the roadside sign says 'Croeso y Cymru', 'Welcome to Wales'.

Index